Natural Born Miracle Makers

Natural Born Miracle Makers

Andrea Ziarno

Copyright ©2017 by Andrea Ziarno

All rights reserved. This book or any portion thereof may not be reproduced or used in any manner whatsoever without the express written permission of the publisher except for the use of brief quotations in a book review.

Printed in the United States of America

First Printing, 2017

ISBN-13: 978-1-945949-94-4

Waterfront Digital Press
2055 Oxford Ave
Cardiff, CA 92007

http://www.waterside.com/

Disclaimer

All content found in this book including: text, images, audio, or other formats were created for informational purposes only. The Content is not intended to be a substitute for professional legal advice or professional medical advice, diagnosis, or treatment. Always seek the advice of your professional legal advisors with any questions you may have regarding a legal matter, and of your physician or other qualified health provider with any questions you may have regarding a medical condition. Never disregard professional legal advice or professional medical advice or delay in seeking either because of something you have read in this publication.

Preface

> "The more wisdom you attain and the more conscious you become, the crazier you will appear to others."
> Albert Einstein

The journey my Soul takes during this lifetime is the same journey Your Soul takes. It is a journey of self-realization and remembering who We All are, The One Soul, The Creator, Unconditional Love. My and Your Soul journey is one that searches for answers to many of Life's mysteries. Who am I? Why am I here? What's the purpose of Life? Was I here before? Was I here with You before? Where am I going after I die? Am I returning after I die? What is the Nature of Reality? Do I create my own reality, and if so, how do I do it? What Laws of Nature govern our daily lives? Is *The Secret*'s Law of Attraction

(Rhonda Byrne, 2006) a real phenomenon? If so, how do I Master its Use?

My Soul journey in travels in Europe, The Americas, North Africa, Asia, and Central and South America over the last 30 years found the answers to these questions which I now share with You. The purpose of sharing my life journey and what I have remembered is to help You to remember who You are, and to make every moment you live a Rich and Happy moment. The tangible results You create from using the wisdom shared with You are rich, real, and absolutely amazing. My experience includes materializing finances, fulfilling relationships, perfect health, luxury consumer goods, travel, and a whole lot more. What I became inside was mirrored back to me by the Universe externally on my journey of Self-realization. In short, I became a Natural-born Miracle Maker. As You read, use and become proficient in the teachings herein. You now become who You already are; A Natural-born Miracle Maker.

This literary work is dedicated to my mother, Czeslawa Ziarno, who passed away in that life at the age of 45, and was reincarnated in a new, beautiful life in 1995 as Ms. Ludmila Panchenko, a Beautiful Soul we have shared many incarnations with in a variety of roles. I thank her for the experiences in all lives we have shared together as Soulmates, and I thank all Souls for the experiences we have shared together.

This book is my gift to You and all the Beautiful Souls I have encountered in my current incarnation as well as in all my previous lives who have returned to Earth in my current lifetime or are soon incarnating. Welcome back, and Blessings of Happiness!

W. Andrea Ziarno, Esq.

Chapter 1

Jesus said, "If your leaders say to you, 'Look, the (Father's) kingdom is in the sky,' then the birds of the sky will precede you. If they say to you, 'It is in the sea,' then the fish will precede you. Rather, the (Father's) kingdom is within you and it is outside you."

    Jesus Christ, The Gospel According to Thomas, Nag Hammadi Library.

WHO AM I? I AM A NATURAL-BORN MIRACLE MAKER, THE CREATOR.

We are All The Creator, The One Soul. I AM YOU, YOU ARE ME, WE ARE ALL THAT WE SEE AND DO NOT SEE, THE ONE SOUL, UNCONDITIONAL LOVE. At our essence we are pure Spirit animating physical forms we call bodies. Full stop as my Italian friends say. We live in this world in the illusion of being separate Souls and distinct physical forms. The illusion extends to all that is material, be it bird, fish, dog, lion, tree, plant, the air, the water, rocks, and so forth. I am Life. It is critical to see beyond this illusion. When you do, a world of pure magic opens up for you in ways that are miraculous to say the least. The magic is the Universe, the rest of You mirroring back to You who You believe and feel You are. No exceptions. If You believe You are less than The Creator, the Universe mirrors back to you this experience. Zero exceptions. If You believe and feel You are the Creator, the Universe Mirrors back to You this experience. And oh, what an exquisite experience it is!

As The Creator, We All are the One Creative Force of the Universe. This fact is profound for it impacts the way You choose to live Life, the thoughts you think, the feelings you feel, the words you speak and the actions you choose to take. Your every thought, emotion, word, and action are part of a creative process that You unleash and are responsible for, either deliberately or unconsciously. This means that You, as The Creator, can call forth any experience you desire using the Natural Law of Creation. It is Your power, Your birthright and Your responsibility to use the Natural Law of Creation to create positive experiences for Yourself and All that is around You, including other people, animals, and indeed the Earth itself. Your end result is 101 percent Guaranteed.

Chapter 2

"Life will give you whatever experience is most helpful for the evolution of your consciousness."

Eckhart Tolle

THE NATURAL LAW OF CREATION: WHAT ARE YOU REALLY CREATING? EXPERIENCES.

As The Creator, You create. In essence, You are creating experiences for Yourself and All those that are around You. The experiences are emotional, and thoughts form experiences and physical experiences based on your interaction with people and objects. For example, if you materialize a luxury Cabrio car, You are not interested in the piece of metal, plastic, glass, and rubber that have been assembled to move You around. The physical form of the car will get old in a period of time, and any car, train or bus can get you from place to place. Rather, the experience is what You wish, and it can take many forms. It is an inner feeling You have from the exterior event of the wind blowing through Your hair and the sun shining on Your face. It is how You feel when Your partner smiles from the seat next to You and holds Your hand. It is the feeling of exhiliration when your foot presses the accelerator to the floor, and the engine vroooms. These experiences for Your happiness and the simultaneous happiness of those around You are high quality creative, emotional experiences. By contrast, if You only have bought and are driving the car to impress others and your ego, you are creating lower vibrational experiences. Both are emotional experiences nonetheless that You have created in a specific moment of time.

All creation of emotional experiences (e.g., happen) in the present moment, in the NOW. It is Your visualization of the experience or experience with the object that serves as the very engine of creation as You call forth the experience to be mirrored back to You in three dimensions. Just sit back for a moment and think how absolutely powerful that truth is and how it impacts how You choose to live Your life. The creation of the emotional experience during the event with the three-dimensional form You desire is always an experience in the now. It is never a past or future experience. Similarly, the creation of objects or three-dimensional forms (when You call them forth) with which You desire an experience, only happens in the now. This holds true at the time You are manifesting and visualizing the three-dimensional form or experience, through a three-dimensional materialization process (in the illusion of time; see e.g., Chapter 3), to the time the 3-D experience or object manifests in Your physical reality.

As soon as You think a thought and feel that You are experiencing the experience with the three-dimensional form, You create it at the non-visible level of creation itself in the present moment. The non-visible level of creation is outside of the limited five-sense field perception. It is a realm that is intangible, yet very, very real. In other words, You cannot see the level of creation with your eyes, touch it, smell it, hear it, feel it with your fingers, yet it exists, in our multi-dimensional reality, the 3-D realm we inhabit being only one of these levels of reality. This is the reason that Jesus Christ taught that if you tell the mountain to move into the sea, and believe it is already done, the three-dimensional event shall occur. Similarly, He taught that if you have bad intentions toward a female, You have already "sinned" against her. He and the others understood that the experience (be it positive or negative) was being created at the level of creation, in that dimension, and that it is mirrored back into three-dimensional experience.

The most important thing You can ever do to manifest a truly happy life is to BE (Feel) that You already are Happiness, Successful (whatever success means to You) notwithstanding what is around You externally. The first step is to "vibe" as Happiness in every moment. In other words, BE that which You wish to experience NOW. This is the state here on earth described by the Eastern sages and mystics as Bliss or Nirvana. This is the reason why the Buddha and other monks and "wholelymen" simply sit under a tree with a smile on their faces. They are happy from within. They have created the experience of happiness from within themselves which is independent of external surroundings or events. They have mastered their "minds." Their minds are the perfect servants of their Divine Souls and no longer run the show of Life.

What You think and feel You are NOW, You experience in this three-dimensional world since You have created it as The Creator. Your thoughts and feelings create the Image of what You wish to experience, knowingly or unknowingly. Since we all are the Creator, in fact ONLY ONE SOUL, we have a responsibility to use the natural law of creation for our highest good, and for the highest good of All around us; in essence US in a different three-dimensional form or costume, if You will. To do otherwise is a misuse of Your inherent power as The Creator and the Natural Law of Creation by the ego, and carries with it Karmic repercussions for Your Soul's experiences, which we describe in later chapters.

Chapter 3

"The only reason for time is so that everything doesn't happen at once."
Albert Einstein

THE TRUE NATURE OF TIME IS THAT "NOW" IS ALL THERE IS; THE "BUFFER" OF TIME IS AN ILLUSION, YET A NECESSARY ONE IN THE MIRACLE MAKING PROCESS.

The concept of "time" as understood by the mind is past, present, and future. The One Soul, Your Soul, only lives in what is REAL, the present. The mind lives in the illusion that is called the past and future. As described in Chapter 2, All creation, including the creation of experiences and the calling forth of objects You desire to have an experience with, happens in the present moment, the NOW. Think of All "time" as a "dot." Think of everything occuring in the "dot" simultaneously, in the NOW. This is the true Nature of Time.

As such, the NOW is all that is real, and all that ever "was" real or all that ever "will be" real is happening NOW. The concept of "infinite time" is really the "dot" of the present moment having various simultaneous overlapping dimensions. You only perceive what You experience NOW. You cannot feel an experience in the past (like a past hurt or a future event) because the concept of "time" is an illusion. It is a "thought" about an event generated by your mind NOW, be it a "past" or "future" event, that triggers an emotion or feeling NOW. Simply put, the past and future are illusions in which no thought or emotion of feeling ever dwells.

The true nature of reality is that All events and experiences described as miracles are occuring simultaneously in the present moment. Any experience You "have" experienced in the illusion of the past or "could ever" experience in the illusion of the future is happening concurrently in the eternal present moment in different overlapping dimensions. This is the reason that many Spiritual Masters have taught that You already are that which You wish to experience NOW, and that it is not necessary to look to the external for that which You wish to experience as it is already within You NOW.

Time is a linear illusion. Science describes the Big Bang as the moment of creation; then billions of years passing, life on earth forming all in a linear manner. This is what we call "mind-foolery in the extreme" and it involves completely living life in an illusory past. Why? The present moment, reality, is a "dot." So the Big Bang is actually happening now in another dimension within the dot of time. Every moment You have ever lived or can ever live is happening simultaneously in the "dot" of time. As applied to Your working miracles, All miracles (experiences and experiences with objects) that could possibly occur, are already occuring NOW once You call them forth in the dot that is time. So, that experience on a luxury yacht or in the luxury home You wish to feel good in with family and friends enjoying a nice glass of vino, enjoying the scent of the sea or forest, already exists in the dot of time, the present moment. How? You are THE CREATOR and can do this easily and effortlessly.

The reason All Spiritual Masters live Life in and teach that You should live Your Life in the present moment, in the "dot" of time, is that they remember the true nature of time. The Spiritual Masters live in reality. To live any other way than in the present moment (e.g., in the illusion of time) is a mistake that the mind makes which causes suffering. In fact, it is the root cause of All suffering anyone has ever experienced. With respect to materializing three-dimensional experiences and experiences with an object, remember that the experience You desire is already done once You call it forth into existence. It exists already within the reality of the present moment, within the "dot" of time. This fact should bring an incredible peace into Your life. Worring about a materialization is the insane domain of a mind that has dragged a Soul out of the reality of the present moment and into the darkness of the illusion of the future. How? The insane mind asks: When will my materialization in three-dimensional form occur? The sane Soul knows that the materialization already exists at the level of creation, and that the three-dimensional experience occurs 100 percent of the time. As such, the Soul is free of suffering, BEing confident of the experience with the three-dimensional materialization.

Why was the illusion of time created by Us All, the One Soul, as an experience during life here on Earth? The reason that the illusion of linear "time" was created was to serve as a buffer and to have an incarnation experience makes sense to the limited faculty of the mind. Remember Your Soul already knows All and is infinite knowledge. Hence, it can digest All events occuring in the dot of time. The mind is a very limited faculty on the other hand, and does not have the bandwidth to digest All things occuring at the same time. The "buffer" of time allows Your mind to make sense of life in the physical realm here on earth by feeding the mind bite-sized pieces of one or more experiences according to "clock time" instead of All experiences at once. The "buffer" of time also serves to safeguard You and others from the instant materialization of All of Your thoughts into physical form. If all of Your mixed 60,000 thoughts You have each day instantly materialized, You and everyone else incarnated around you here on earth would sit on a pile of chaotic garbage e.g., a mess. You think you wish to have a dog, a Great Dane. The Great Dane materializes on Your Couch. Then You wish 59,999 other objects the same day and all materialize. Well, You have one cluttered house in 24-hours which serves no one's interest.

We All as The Creator also created a buffer of "time" which is flexible and works to Your advantage in the materialization process. It first permits You a window (albiet an illusory window since Your thought has created an experience in an alternate simultaneous reality happening now to You) from thought to three-dimensional mirroring back to You of the experience in this reality to: 1) change Your selection, and 2) to enjoy a physical process that includes action steps for a specific materialization. In other words, You have "time" to create or change Your selection. Your thought about an elephant in Your living room does not instantly materialize here on earth causing You and Your family a great mess. You enjoy the actions of choosing, designing, molding, building or painting a vase or a house with Your hands, and enjoy the finished product when complete. You enjoy the process of each brush stroke when creating a painting until the finished product unfolds. You enjoy the process of creating music and singing the final song.

How do I manage (modulate) the "buffer" of time to my advantage when materializing an experience or an experience with an object? Strong Emotions, any kind, coupled with the thought accelerate the image appearing as Your 3-D reality. Think of your thought visualization as a Jet flying to a destination which can fly at different speeds depending on what type of fuel is put into its gas tank e.g., low energy fuel, medium energy fuel, and ultra-fast, high energy fuel. Remember that Your emotions (how You feel) at the moment of the visualization are the fuel that determines which fuel is used that sets the flight speed of your Jet (of Your 3-D materializations) e.g., the fuel type determines how fast your Jet flies to its materialization destination. Slow low energy emotions e.g., apathy, result in retarded, slow materializations. Half-hearted feelings e.g., you feel like being in the experience in a luke warm manner, result in materializations in three dimensions taking a longer "time." Very powerful high energy emotions of any kind e.g., a Deep Happiness, Laughter, Euphoria, Soulgasms, supercharge the three-dimensional appearance of experiences or objects for the experience, and compress the "illusion" of time substantially. The more "UUUUUUMMMMMMPFFFFFF" powering the thought form, the faster You experience the three-dimensional materialization.

Hence, it is important to be aware of what You are thinking when You are emotionally charged e.g., either postively or negatively. Why? The mirroring back to You of what You are thinking while being emotionally charged happens "fast." So it is important to train your mind like an Olympic Athlete to ONLY, I REPEAT ONLY, generate thoughts that are for Your Best and Highest Good, and for the Best and Highest Good of All around You, in All present moments, especially emotionally charged present moments. In the same vein, while You and everyone around You is positively charged, visualize (create) experiences that include optimal materializations for Your happiness and the happiness of All those around You simultaneously. A delightful idea is to have a periodic materialization party with those who remember the principles of materialization and are aligned with that which You wish to materialize. All vibe high with Happiness.

The party harnesses powerful group energies and accelerates the materialization process for all through this Spiritual Teamwork practice which is described in more detail in subsequent chapters.

Chapter 4

"What you give to others, you give to yourself. Equally, what you fail to give to others, you fail to give to yourself."
Neale Donald Walsch

MATERIALIZE FOR THE HAPPINESS OF ALL, THE ONE SOUL; MATERIALIZE FOR THE WHOLE, NOT ONLY PARTS OF THE WHOLE.

There are strong empaths that love to serve, materialize and make other people happy, to the exclusion of their own happiness. You see this in many examples of the "doting" mother with children. She does all for the benefit of her children while doing little for her own happiness.

This is a mistake. On the flip side of the coin, there are egomaniacs that love to materialize only for the happiness of themselves. This is also a mistake. Neither the empath nor the egomaniac serve the best and highest good of The One Soul, All of us. The empath has forgotten about herself/himself. The egomaniac has forgotten about All others. Examples of egomaniacs run the spectrum from the doting middle-class mother, the career politician, the World leader, to the unhappy egomaniac billionairess/billionaire. Both the pure empath and the egomaniac's approaches to materialization and life experiences are flawed. Each forgets about the experience of one or more parts of The One Soul, Us All.

By way of example, think of the egomaniacal classic "gold-digging" masked woman who wishes to be a millionaire. She does her visualization of having a million dollars. A rich suitor appears who is a millionaire. The materialization is proceeding through three-dimensional process, yet she is still only thinking about herself. She gets pregnant and marries him, yet he soon dies from a heart attack in bed while they are making love. Her wish comes true, yet she becomes a rich widow, her husband is dead, and her child is now fatherless. Clearly, this is an example of a substandard materialization because All parts of the Whole are not served, and while her materialization appeared, suffering was created as a result of the materialization since All parts of the whole were not considered while materializing.

In addition to empaths and egomaniacs, personality types can be classified as introvert or extrovert. The author suggests there is a better variant. BE AN ALLTROVERT. An ALLTROVERT is a person who is an Introvert and an Extrovert simultaneously. The person is an introvert since She/He enjoys spending time allone, with Her/His Highest Self. The person is an extrovert since She/He enjoys spending time with others, experiencing HerSelf/His/Self in another physical form. The Alltrovert is Whole, the Oneness. When a person is only an Introvert, only an Extrovert, only an empath, or only an egomaniac, the person is not Whole. An Alltrovert materializes for the Whole.

What is the the optimal Life experience and materialization? It is quite simple really. First, Love Your Self enough to include Your happiness in the experience and materialization. Simultaneously, Love the others to include their happiness in the experience and materialization. Spend time Allone, with Your Self. Spend time with others. This results in the Whole, The One Soul, us All benefiting from the materialization and experience.

Materializations for the Wholeness simultaneously are the optimal approach for the highest good. Again, Wholeness materializations are those for Your Happiness and for the Happiness of All around You at the same time. These materializations are complete and optimal materializations since all parts of The One Soul, including You, are being served up delights and being satisfied in the delights. Think of a young billionaire who is adept at materializing at scale. He uses the forces of the Universe for the benefit of himself (He loves himself in a healthy way sans ego) and the benefit of All others at the same time e.g., business partners, artists, family, friends,"strangers," and the World as a Whole. He enjoys a luxury lifestyle while at the same time sharing his abundance with All around him. This is the way to materialize as a Natural-born Miracle Maker.

Chapter 5

"You create your own universe as you go along."

                                  Winston Churchill

THE "I AM" NATURE OF REALITY AND THE "I AM" CREATION PRINCIPLE.

One of Your purposes in Life is really very simple. Your purpose is to remember "Who You Are." So who are You? During our life journey we posed this question to young and old we met all across Europe. The answers people gave, except for a handful, were mundane, and failed to answer the question. In response to the question, the answers many gave included an association with a role they have in life or part of their life history e.g., the place where they were born—e.g., I am from Zurich, Kiev, etc. Others identified their roles in life as describing who they are: I am a doctor, student, mother, father, etc. After listening to the responses, we smiled at the person we were speaking to and said: "Now I will tell You who You are? Ready? You are not the role you have chosen in Life. You are not defined by the place where you live or were born, or Your Nationality. You are the Creator, The One Soul, Unconditional Love, and All You see around You is You in a different costume." The Truth we shared with many resonated with their Souls, as the gleam in their eyes and the smile on their faces indicated. There were also others we encountered who were very heavily conditioned (think Pavlov's dog). These included a Ukrainian Orthodox priest and Mormon missionaries plying their trade on the streets of Kiev.

The encounter with the Orthodox priest was particularly amusing. He appeared before Us twice within a matter of a couple of hours so we took this as a cue from the Universe to meet him. During the second time he appeared, we posed him the question above, and gave him the truthful response sharing with Him that he is God in a black hat costume. His ego jumped out after our smiling response to him, and with fire and brimstone in his eyes he blurted out to us in Russian: "I am not God and You are not God." We smiled at him and thought, "Man, you are full of shit." Not wishing to have him smash us over the head with the heaving cross he was wearing around his neck, we decided to wish him a happy day and walked away. A similar encounter happened with the two Mormon young men, what they call Mormon missionaries. These are well-dressed and groomed young men with a decent vibe and smiling faces.

However, we discovered that they are heavily conditioned. They responded to the question like robots reciting chapter and verse from the Book of Mormon, which we term: "The Book of Moron" amusingly. Both responses are mistakes. Be it faux Christianity, Judiasm, or Islam, All of these religions teach a lie. The lie is that we are all something smaller and stupider than The Creator e.g., children of God, sheep being led by a Shepard, etc. The lie is also that God is somewhere outside of Us. For the faux Christians, God is in heaven. For the Jews, God sits in an Ark, or they pray to a stone wall. For the Muslims, God is somewhere on the floor or above the floor, so they engage in prayer ceromonies worshipping the floor, and bowing to it three times a day.

So now ask Your Self, Who I AM? Stop for a moment and let Your Soul provide the answer without any thought. Here is the Answer that Your Soul gives You: You are You and All that You see and do not see around You, is You. You are The One Soul, Unconditional Love. You are The Alpha and Omega in the present moment. At this point, You are having a "Wholely" moment (being holy means you have a hole, something is missing). You are Being whole with All that is around You. And now the author shares with You an easy WAY to remember this fact. Who You are is described in the words: "I AM." "I AM" is the Biblical name for God from the Old Testament, YOU, and All You see around You. Also appearing in the Old Testament is the phrase: "I AM THAT I AM" that means that You are the other person, that tree, that animal, and that object, everything, and they are You. There is no difference between You and everything else, but for the costumes. Take off the costumes, and **WE ALL SEE WE ARE THE ONE SOUL, THE CREATOR.** Everything physical that You See is Spirit, The One Soul, condensed into matter. Some of the matter is animated e.g., people, animals, plants, fish, microbes. Some of the matter is inanimate e.g., not animated. Some moves around e.g., is animated. I AM THAT I AM describes the UNITY of All creation and the fact that All creation is a manifestation of THE ONE SOUL, US ALL, in a myriad of costumes, and physical forms.

Why is it important to remember Who You are in the miracle making process? Again, the answer is simple. Remember that You are the Creator of All, and You create All that You wish. Forget that You are the Creator e.g., think that You are less than the Creator as the faux Christians, Jews, and Muslims would have you believe, and You "self-limit" Your ability to create miracles. To use our Chicago French, you mindfool yourself or you permit someone else to mindfool you. For example, only thinking that Jesus was a Son of God, and only He has the power to save You and work miracles in Your life, results in You forgetting that You Your Self are the Creator and robs you of the power to create. The Universe, the rest of Us, does not care about the experience You ultimately wish to create since Your Soul has the gift of Freewill here on planet Earth. As such, You are free to believe that You are less than the Creator and You have that experience mirrored back to You. The large scale mindfoolery of the major religions is that they have bamboozled billions of incarnated Souls over thousands of years to think that they are less than The Creator. You may ask why was this done? The answer is again simple.

Control. Business. Cash. If you have a ruling religious elite who wishes to control incarnated Souls, they lie to them and have them believe that they are less than God. Second, have the sheep believe that they have only one life, one incarnation, and depending on whether or not they have paid their tithes, indulgences, kissed your ring, bowed to you, come to your services and/or been faithful slaves or not, You lie to them and tell them they are going to a heaven or a hell. Rob them of the most important knowledge ("gnosis") of their natural-born Self, The Creator, animating a physical form.

Having identified the lies of "establishment" religons, we now have now set the table for the "faithful" to basically unmindfool themselves and recapture their innate power e.g., remember that They All are the Creator, and remind them that they each inherently possess infinite powers of creation. This is a major milestone in the process of BEING the Natural-born Miracle Makers You already are. We speak in this work of the materialization of three-dimensional objects and experiences. Yet, the true depth of Who we really are is much, much more breathtaking than miracles worked on earth illustrate, or that that can be described with the limitations words impose on information exchange. Imagine this. You de-animate Your physical form and return to the Spirit realm. You are THE CREATOR. What can You choose to do from there? The answer to this question is startling. Create Anything. This means that You can create other Universes with Your unlimited power as The Creator. You can create other physical, beautiful life forms that You and other Souls can animate. You can split Your Self into other Souls, All Part of the One Soul, in yet new unknown ways for the One Soul to see and experience itself. There is zero limit on What You can create in Your form as Spirit. Similarly, believe that there is zero limit on what experiences you may materialize while You are animating a physical form here on Earth and it is done. The Truth is told, and the Truth is bold.

The term "I AM" as applied to Creating Life Experiences for You also means Intention/Wish Action Manifestion/Materialization (3-D Realization of the wish/intention). While the creation of life experiences also involves the manifestation of physical objects for You and others around You to enjoy, it is not the object that is of primary interest to you, it is the experience with the object as we have shared with You earlier. As one of our enlightened friends, Achim, has shared with us: "If you own too many objects, there is a risk the objects may own you." Jesus Christ taught: "Be in the World, but not of it." These statements are profound and deserve an observation. The object manifestation is not the end game. The end game is the experience with the object. When the object has served its purpose of serving Your best and highest good and that of all around you, freely and easily release the object to serve someone else. Let the object bring Happiness to someone else's life. A delightful case in point involved our arrival in Kiev in January of 2017 in minus 30-degree Celcius temperatures. We were wearing two down jackets, a lighter Patagonia jacket, a heavier, longer down coat, a warm wool hat, scarf, leather gloves, and weather proof wool lined Swiss boots. This abundance of clothing kept us warm in the inclement Ukrainian winter for about two weeks, and served us well. As we travelled the metro in Kiev, a number of homeless people were living in the metro underground. In terms of materializations, these folks were there to give us examples of the life experience not to materialize e.g., that of lack and poverty.

Having a wild eye for bringing random acts of kindness to the world, we decided that it's time to share the abundance that found its way our direction, so as we walked to the metro we systematically shed the extras, while at the same time we kept enough of the clothing on to remain comfortable. First, we stopped for a smoke and saw a man directly across from us. Off came the larger down jacket as we walked across the metro underground and presented it to him. His eyes sparkled as we handed him the warm jacket. We just felt all good about being able to help the man keep warm, with zero expectation of receiving anything in return from him.

"All that you give is a gift. All that you receive is a gift. Everything else is a trade," said Achim. Similarly, the intention behind our giving the gift is important. The gifts were given with the intention of unconditional love. The gifts were charged therefore with positive energy. The same events continued for the morning with us being left with the one Patagonia winter jacket and a pair of dress shoes. It was a wonderful experience for me and for all those who enjoyed the presents. The realization was that All the others were Us in another costume, so the gift I received for myself was a warm happy feeling. The gift that I gave was a tangible object that kept the others warm. There was zero trade involved as all was given in unconditional love with zero expectation of receiving anything in return. I created a brilliant life experience for All in that moment that I share with You Now. These are the examples of random acts of kindness we all can enjoy in every moment. Zero mind activity, just the Soul expressing itself and creating Happy experiences for All. The objects are of zero significance, the experience is All significant and the materialization worthwhile. As a Natural-born Miracle Maker You are adept at materializing more on demand.

Chapter 6

"Our intention creates our reality."
　　　　　　　　　　Dr. Wayne Dyer

VISION BOARDS FOR VISUALIZATION OF YOUR WISHES USING THE "I AM" LAW OF NATURE; ORDERING WITH SPECIFICITY.

Our attention is focused on the practical nuts and bolts of the the materialization process using the "I AM" LAW OF NATURE. The nuts and bolts include the use of vision boards to laser focus Your Intention/Wish into an exact, concrete Image to Manifest/Materialize. Hold the vision board image in your mind and visualize that You are already in the image, feeling and experiencing that which is portrayed in the image with your five physical senses e.g., every sight, smell, sensation on your skin, taste, etc. This places Your order with the Universe in a way that is very, very specific.

　　Think of Yourself being in at an Italian Pizza Restaurant. There is a menu. The menu has a variety of menu items e.g., 25 different pizzas to select from. Yet, You tell your server, I wish a Pizza. The server does not know if she or he should bring you a Pepperoni Pizza, a Margherita or Hawaiian Style Pizza. Your order was not specific enough in this example at the restaurant.

The same law holds true with the Universe, The rest of You, The One Soul. If you make a general wish e.g., I wish a car, the Universe does not know what specific car and experience therewith you have called forth. Should it rearrange itself for you to bring you a Maserati, Bentley, Jaguar, Volkswagen, Audi, Seat, or Fiat? The result is that the Universe may deliver you a 1964 Oldsmobile. It is a car. You asked for a car. The Universe delivered. Yet, this was not the end result that would have brought you maximum happiness.

A linchpin in the materialization process is "Specificity." First, know exactly the experience You wish to materialize. Not knowing what You wish to experience is fatal. Nothing will be experienced, except for what comes Your direction from other sources. Being vague also does not serve You. The more specific you are about what you wish to enjoy, the more specific order You have placed with the Universe. Having placed a specific, well-defined order with the Universe, the waiter knows what to tell the chef to prepare for You. The request/end result must be specific for Your materialization, the end result, to be as You desire.

A real world example of how to be specific is in the case of Mohamed who we met in Odessa, Ukraine walking down the street. Mohammed is a young architect from Egypt who was in the spring of 2017 separated from his young wife and their baby girl. As Mohamed and I enjoyed a coffee, he told me about how much he loved his wife and daughter and how much he wished to be reunited with them. The young man was in tears as he described his separation. We instantly decided this was a call to action on our part. First, we told Mohamed about the vision boarding process, and how thoughts fueled with emotion result in 3-D materializations.

Mohamed was intrigued by the process. We requested that he send us a photo to our iPhone of him and his family together during happy times. The reason they split was because both he and she were engaged in the relationship at the level of mindfoolery. This resulted in fights, needless quarrels, and ultimately a split-up. We told Mohamed that business as usual in terms of the mindfoolery on his part and her part, and the living in the past e.g. he said, she said, he did, she did that to me, stops. Then we took the image of the family in happy times and inserted a spell in text onto the image: I AM MOHAMED,

IRINA, AND JULIA, HAPPILY REUNITED AS A FAMILY FOR THE BEST AND HIGHEST GOOD OF ALL BY THE END OF APRIL 2017. We sent the image to Mohamed with instructions that he visualize the reunion and continual happy times together. We also shared the image with others in our Soul family to further energize the materialization. Two months later I get a call from Mohamed on a return trip to Odessa. I ask him about his family reunion materialization. Mohamed tells me that Irina and his baby girl have returned to him, and that now they again enjoy a happy family life again.

"Specificity" is part of the 33 powerful process steps using vision boards to focus Your power of creation properly to materialize the exact object and experience with the object You desire. THE 33 PROCESS STEPS LASER BEAM FOCUS YOUR WISH/REQUEST BY SELECTING THE EXACT OBJECT AND EXPERIENCE WITH THE OBJECT YOU WISH TO MATERIALIZE. As we move forward with the material in this book, You note that we are typing in both upper and lower case letters in what appears to be an unconventional format. The use of upper and lower case lettering came into use early in the first millenium in Europe. It was a break from the traditional way of writing which only involved the use of a single upper case. You see this in traditional Greek, Roman, and Eastern languages. In our view, the invention of upper and lower case lettering only serves to exacerbate the separation. I AM big, You are small, if you will. In conventional modern day electronic message exchange, use of upper case lettering has taken on the meaning of shouting. This is not the case in this book. Rather, we are moving back to the traditional way of writing which involves the use of a single, upper case. In this way, even our writing and the writing of others moves back into a theme of singularity, oneness. Us All being ONE SOUL, not ONE BIG SOUL, and other smaller souls. For NOW, we use the old way combined with the not so old way of writing.

As described, AN INITIAL PROCESS STEP IS TO FIND AN IMAGE/PICTURE THAT MATCHES THE SPECIFIC EXPERIENCE YOU WISH AND FIRST VISUALIZE. The relevance of the image is that it is the form in which the experience can be had at the time of three-dimensional mirroring of Your visualization. Own the visualization and experience that the object provides You. That means make it your own. Specify the detail. Feel it NOW. For example, where You wish to manifest an experience with an automobile e.g., a BMW, Mercedes, Ferrari, Jaguar, Bentley, Rolls Royce, Maserati, etc., specify all features of the automobile. The process is made easy and fun now with the automatic car manufacturer configurators available online. With respect to specific materializations the author is proceeding with, the author has taken specific action steps aligned with the visualizations and materializations.

A case in point, the author desired to materialize a personal Bentley and a company Rolls Royce. To assist in the visualization with all five senses, the author proceeded to the Bentley and Rolls Royce dealership in Zurich, Switzerland. There the author spent an enjoyable couple of hours configuring the specific automobiles for manifesting the experience. The process involved picking and choosing all features of the autos including models, exterior and interior furnishings, and custom features the author enjoys such as a bespoke water pipe in the interior and company logos on the interior seating. Then the author sat in the models on the showroom floor. There he closed his eyes and smelled the new car leather interior, felt the exquisite supple leather on the seats, and grasped the steering wheel in hand, and felt that he was driving and being chauffeured in the exact autos of his choosing. The visualization was supplemented with actually being in and owning the autos. The experience was superb. This cemented the image in the realm of creation for what was to be mirrored in 3-D reality for the author and all those around him.

Actions must also be aligned with the visualization and are required process steps, so the author proceeded to obtain a contract for ordering the specific car, and obtaining the bank wire payment slips and filling them in with the purchase price of the automobiles. There was zero haggling about the price. Why? The actions were aligned to have the dealership be happy with the sale of a profitable automobile, and more importantly, the author sent a signal to the Universe that the funds are already there to pay the full purchase price of the automobiles. All was done in perfect alignment with the visualization. The author then proceeded to create custom corporate license plates for the automobiles reflecting the author's new companies with the corporate brand "I AM." Next, the Universe started delivering the synchronicities/synchrodestinies for the specific materializations which were simply miraculous. For example, the author was at a consulate picking up a replacement passport for one that was lost during his travels. Outside the consulate stood a white car with the license plate "I AM" just as in the vision/visualization boards the author had created. The synchornicities were put in place by the universe, the owner of the white car, being where the author was synchronously, to inform the author that his visualization is proceeding to 3-D manifestation. Next step, the author is in the cars enjoying them in 3-D form, both driving them himself and being chauffeured with those in his Soul family and friends.

Choosing to Share in the abundance the author was creating with members of his Soul family, the author then desired to present automobiles to members of his Soul family. Specifically, the author wished to present a white Maserati GranCabrio to his beloved partner, and other luxury automobiles to other beloveds. In 2014, the wish for the Maserati was sent into Universal consciousness without the desired specificity. The Universe logged the wish and was proceeding with the 3-D materialization after both the author's beloved and the author energized the visualization. In Odessa, the author and his beloved were preparing for a photosession with a makeup artist. The author went outside the hotel Ekaterina in Odessa and low and behold the Universe delivered a synchrodestiny (described in later chapters for the materialization) that included a burgundy Maserati GranTurismo standing outside of the hotel entrance door. The author noted the message to his beloved, and we proceeded with the photosession.

When the author arrived in Switzerland, the author proceeded with the specific action steps to have the visualization proceed accurately. Having noted that more specificity was required, the author then selected an image with exactly the car he wished to present to his beloved and configured the car online down to the last detail. In this step of the process, the author proceeded to the family-owned Maserati dealership in St. Gallen, Switzerland, and went through the visualization process described above for the Bentley and Rolls Royce. Now the appropriate level of specificity was in place for the Universe to deliver the order. Practically speaking there are a variety of online tools that make the visualization with specifity process fun and enjoyable. These include the use of apps that apply text to your image and also meme generators. USE A MEME GENERATOR OR TEXT APPLICATION APP TO CREATE TEXT THAT REFLECTS THE EXACT EXPERIENCE WITH THE OBJECT. THE MATERIALIZATION OF THE EXPERIENCE, AND TEXT SHOULD BE EXACT: I AM (NAME(S)) AND I (WE) CALL FORTH ENJOYING (WHO, WHAT, WHEN, AND WHERE). In this way, you focus Your thoughts and feelings for the visualization experience. FOR ALL VISION BOARDS, CAST A SPELL BY ADDING THE WORDS/SPELL: "…TO SERVE THE BEST AND HIGHEST GOOD OF MY SOUL, ALL THE SOULS AROUND ME, AND ALL CREATION. SO IT IS DONE."

What are spells? Spells are real white magic that calls forth specific experiences. Verbal and written Spells marshall the forces of the rest of You, THE ONE SOUL, to assist Your materialization 3-D process. The word spell itself also refers to the letters used to create a word. Words are the subject matter or content of the spell that provides the specificity for the visualization. Spells are an integral part of the process of aligning thought (intangible form of energy), feeling (tangible form of energy), with the spoken word (audible form of energy perceptible by the human ear or an instrument). Historically, the practice of spelling or casting spells has been denigrated as being something dark and the practice of witches. This is bullshit. White spells are powerful positive tools in the materialization process. Spells are cast on objects and people and are useful for materializations. Spells affect the way You and others around You, including people, places, and things, interact with You to effectuate the materialization process. They are to be ONLY used for good results as described above because of the Karmic blowback effects described in later chapters of this book. The word "Abracadabra" is taken from the Kabbalah and simply means "As I speak, I call forth." Remember that All thoughts manifest, and spells are useful tools for the visualization and materialization process. When using the Good spell described above, You ensure that the process creates optimal Karma for You and the most enjoyable process for the rest of You, All others.

An example of a spell that materialized related to the Maserati GranCabrio materialization involved the Vice President of Marketing of Maserati Switzerland. At the dealership in St. Gallen, Switzerland, the visualization was complete and the kind daughter of the family owner instantly offered to introduce us to the Vice President of Marketing for Maserati Switzerland, and offered us two complimentary tickets to the Zurich autoshow which was to transpire in about 3 weeks from the date the author was at the dealership. The author proceeded to take action and contact the Maserati executive, actions were aligned with the materialization by email correspondence. The Maserati executive proposed a meeting at the Zurich autoshow later in the month and three days prior to the meeting he set, he sent an email excusing himself due to corporate obligations at the autoshow. The author then proceeded to cast a positive spell (another application of the I AM principle) so that the meeting procede as originally set by the Maserati executive. The author then proceeded to the Zurich autoshow, and to the very well done Maserati booth there. At the booth, the author asked if the Maserati executive was attending. The kind, professional staff said, yes, and called him to meet us. We met with him to discuss business successfully and to proceed with the next steps in the materialization as well as to discuss related film product placement business with Maserati. The spell worked and what ultimately happened is the Universe rescheduled the Maserati executive's other business commitments in such a way that our meeting could proceed for the best and highest good of all. Next process step in the materialization complete.

Another example of how powerful spell casting is, using the I AM principle really, relates to this author's materialization of the world's largest personal and business luxury mega-yacht called *The Absolute,* which is also the title of one of the I AM STUDIO PRODUCTIONS AG films in a feature film quadrilogy. This mega-yacht carries a message of truth to the world about who we all are and has painted on both of its sides the Truth: I AM UNCONDITIONAL LOVE. So here is how the spell casting proceeded. The author requested that his yacht desginer from Norway living in California proceed with the vision board for the vessel. It was completed and sent over to the author. The author then requested his yacht designer to tell him who could construct a 612-foot (212-meter) vessel in Europe. The yacht designer said there were two companies with these capabilities e.g., Luerssen in Bremen, Germany and Blohm & Voss in Hamburg, Germany.

The author had not yet contacted either company about the vessel build so neither company knew about the project. During a meditation on a Friday morning in early September, the author sent the request into Universal consciousness to meet the decision makers of one of the yacht builders and the request for guidance regarding which yacht builder to travel to. In the silence, the author felt Hamburg was the direction to travel to. At 9:00 am on a Friday morning, the author boarded a Swiss train in the direction of Hamburg. Three stops from Hamburg, the author met a pretty young blonde girl named Isabella and we chatted about the projects and cinema releases, and each went our separate ways. Remember her name. It was the Universe sending a synchrodestiny for *The Absolute* yacht 3-D completion by 2022.

Arriving at the office of Blohm & Voss at 6:00 pm on a Friday evening, the author asked the two German security guards to speak to someone about the yacht build and project. A kind guard got on the phone and after five minutes gave the phone to us. The name of the Blohm & Voss sales executive was Isabella. Another logged synchrodestiny. Isabella informed us that she was in Paris at the moment to move into her new apartment. We requested a new meeting date option or asked whether someone else could meet with us. She got back on the phone, and the phone was given to us again. Isabella then told us that we would meet with the President and Chief Financial Officer of Blohm & Voss in their offices upstairs in five minutes. The meeting then proceeded successfully. The spell was successful and the wish materialized within 12 hours.

Chapter 7

"Karma has no menu. You get served what you deserve."
                    Power of Positivity

THE LAW OF KARMA; THE MATERIALIZATION PROCESS AND KARMIC BLOWBACK.

How does the Natural Law of Karma interface with the Natural Law of Creation and the materialization process? From the level of The One Soul, the Laws that govern our incarnation experience here on earth govern our interactions with each other, and our decisions and materializations all work within the framework of these Laws. We All, as a Collective, The One Soul, in its different illusory forms have put in place these Natural Laws for incarnation experiences here on earth. These are the rules of the game we have chosen to play under together. The Law of Karma is a Law of Nature, and one of these sets the rules of the game. Understand the Laws of

Nature, and You understand the game of Life. Understand the game of Life, and use the Laws of Nature, and You and All around You win the game of Life. You work what appear to be miracles to other people, but are just everyday magic you enjoy.

Since We are All the One Soul in the illusion of being separate creatures, that which You wish for another person, animal, etc., You are actually wishing for Yourself. Jesus Christ remembered this Law of Nature and shared its meaning with us in his statement: "That which you do unto others, you do unto me." He understood that the other was Himself, and that He was the Other, since we ultimately are only the One Soul. In the same vein, American Author, Neale Donald Walsch, in his epic work, *Conversations with God,* states: "There is only one person in the room." He remembered that we are also The One Soul, in the illusion of being separate Souls and separate physical forms. This means that whatever thoughts, feelings, words or actions you have directed towards another Soul (again, the Soul being another person, animal, plant, tree, fish, or the earth), you are thinking feeling, speaking, and acting on Your Self. The same holds true for casting spells and wishing something onto the other. As a result of the natural law of Karma, All of Your intentions, speech, actions, and materializations have a Karmic blowback effect. The blowback effect appears as a manifestation of the same or similar experience or event in Your Life experience through people, places, and events.

Positive intentions, speech, actions, and materializations have a positive Karmic blowback effect for You in your current life or a future life. The same holds true for the opposite intentions, speech, actions, and materializations across Your lifetimes.

A true story now comes to mind. The author was dating and living with a beautiful young girl from Dnepropetrovsk, Ukraine while she was attending Law School there for two years. Her name is Alina (more about Her Soul and her previous incarnation as the author's childhood best friend in the Natural Law of Reincarnation chapter in this book). Alina has a first cousin named Arthur. Arthur at that time was about nine or 10 years old. Arthur's obsession was playing computer games with his friends online to the exclusion of all other activities including going to school for lessons. Arthur is an actor and choose to lie to his parents thinking up excuses of being ill with tummy aches and other maladies all in a ruse not to attend classes, stay at home and play his computer games nonstop. Arthur was lost in the computer game. Arthur was creating Karma for himself with his ruse. "Be careful what you wish for, it comes true." Arthur's energy was directed at staying home and creating fake illnesses to accomplish this end result for himself. Arthur's parents, a gynecologist and a police officer, were listening to Arthur's stories and focusing their energy on what he was saying, adding fuel to this Karmic fire. Arthur's Aunt Alla and two grandparents were adding more Karmic fuel to this fire with thought and emotion focusing on Arthur's ruse. Well, the shit hit the fan one day in September and the energy focus by all involved created a Karmic event for Arthur.

Arthur was playing on a swing with one of his gamer friends, and he flew off the swing and broke both of his arms. The result was that he had both of his arms in casts for several weeks, stayed at home, but was not able to play computer games because of the casts. The Karmic event happened due to the wishes of his family members that he not play computer games and Arthur's energy focus that he stay at home. Both Arthur and his family got their wishes granted in the example shown here. Huge collective family energies were behind this materialization.

The process, the broken arms and the hospitalization, were Karmic events based on the wishes of All. The moral of this true story is, "Be careful what you wish for the other, wishes come true." This is another example of how one must be careful when focusing emotionally charged energy and thought on the other. The best process to use is to be informed and add: "for the best and highest good for all" when one is involved in situations similar to this one.

This is an example of Karmic blowback in a single lifetime with a group of family members. However, the Karmic blowback effect may also span across lifetimes or incarnations since all Natural Laws interact with one another, and time is an illusion. In other words, since Reincarnation is a Law of Nature along with The Law of Karma, the lesson to remember is to ONLY create positive Karma for Yourself and others in All lifetimes. Creating positive Karma for Yourself is mirrored back to You in Your current lifetime and in future lifetimes.

Chapter 8

"The mind and the body are like parallel universes. Anything that happens in the mental Universe must leave tracks in the physical one."

> Dr. Deepak Chopra

THE NATURAL LAW OF MIRRORING AND MATERIALIZATION USING THE VISION BOARDING PROCESS.

Since You are the Creator, where Your attention and awareness goes, Your energy, the energy of the Creator goes. You are All infinite beings, so in essence you direct infinite amounts of energy into what You put Your attention on continuously. One way to provide a continuum of energy flow into a materialization is to place your vision boards where they catch your attention, and hence direct your energy All the time. Many authors such as Jack Canfield in *The Secret* film (2006) describe examples of placing a $100,000 vision board bill on the ceiling above his bed so that when he rises it's the first thing that his attention and energy is directed to. This method is highly successful and Jack explains his materialization of $92,000 within a year as a result of focusing his attention on the end result continuously. This was repeated by a $1,000,000 USD materialization for a book advance which resulted in the wonderful *Chicken Soup for the Soul* book written by Jack. For each of You, it is effective to PRINT OUT YOUR VISION BOARD(S) AND PUT THEM IN A PLACE YOU SEE THEM ALL THE TIME. IN THIS WAY, YOUR ATTENTION IS FOCUSED ON THE END RESULT YOU HAVE INTENDED TO 3-D MATERIALIZE.

NEXT, "CALL FORTH" THE EXPERIENCE WITH YOUR THOUGHTS, FEELINGS, AND SPOKEN WORDS IN A VISUALIZATION. ALL THE TOOLS YOU USE ARE IN ALIGNMENT IN THIS WAY. Once you have Mastered what you wish to think about and have replaced all low vibrational thoughts with thoughts of a high vibration, You change the way You feel and what You speak about. That which You speak about also affects the visualization. Your thoughts become words when you wish to speak and the words place further energy into that which You experience. In other words, that which You think about, You speak about.

The selection of the appropriate words in your visualization process is significant. We have observed that many who dabble in the art of materialization on Instagram, tend to be very sloppy with their words, and hence, very sloppy with the spells they cast. This also holds true for many public figures who have quotes attributed to them which then hundreds of thousands of people energize when they repeat what was publicly broadcast. An example of this is the mistaken use of the word "want." I want to be loved. I want a car. I want a boat. I want to be rich. These are the wrong words to use and energize. Why? The Universe, the rest of You, understands the word want as meaning that you "lack" something. So the ultimate effect is the opposite effect from having that which is called forth. The user of such words experiences the "lack" of that which follows the use of the word want. In other words, the Universe mirrors back "lack" to the user. This is the opposite result of that which is intended.

The correct use of words in the materialization process includes the words: "I CALL FORTH." This is a perfect use of Your divine power with aligned wording to bring the experience to three-dimensional realization. After "calling forth" the experience or object for an experience, FEEL YOU ARE ALREADY HAVING THE EXPERIENCE NOW. We have described in earlier Chapters that only the present moment is real, so when You call it forth AND FEEL

IT IS DONE, it is done at the level of creation NOW. BE THERE IN THE EXPERIENCE NOW WITH ALL THE SENSATIONS THE EXPERIENCE AFFORDS. AT THIS POINT, YOU HAVE CREATED THE EXPERIENCE AT THE LEVEL OF CREATION THROUGH YOUR DIVINE CREATIVE SOUL, AND THE UNIVERSE MIRRORS THE EXPERIENCE BACK TO YOU IN 3-D FORM AS A RESULT OF THE NATURAL LAW OF MIRRORING. Jesus Christ understood the Natural Law of Mirroring and summed it up in the simple words: "As above (in the realm of creation), so below (on earth in 3-D form)."

The benefit of the vision boarding/visualization process and being in the experience NOW is a two for one effect. You have the feeling of the experience a minimum of two times: 1) at the point of visualization, and 2) at the time of the 3-D materialization. Your mind and body equate both as one in the same experience. Imagination (image in action) is everything. There are numerous studies where athletes are asked to run a marathon only in their imagination. Medical equipment records that their muscles are firing in the same manner as if they are physically running the marathon. This also gets us to the meaning of the word: imagination. It means "image in action" and should be more properly spelled in the Dictionary as "imageinaction" to completely understand the meaning of the word. The "image" is the thought form of the experience you wish to materialize. The "in action" has three meanings: 1) the image is in action since you feel you are already taking action in the image; 2) you take action to achieve your materialization; and 3) the image you hold in your head ultimately becomes a 3-D "in action" experience for You, which is always the case. The "image" and the "in action" part creates a feeling. The feeling is that which You wish to experience. In other words, what really matters to You is how you feel at any present moment in the experience, and the visualization creates the feeling You wish, activates the Natural Law of Mirroring, and then You feel the experience once again in three-dimensional form. How You feel at any moment is an imprint You make on **THE ONE SOUL, YOU, THE REST OF US** e.g., **THE COLLECTIVE** consciousness. Ultimately, the rest of You, **THE REST OF THE ONE SOUL** says, okay this is how You wish to feel, so I will mirror back to You, Me, more of the same.

Chapter 9

"Soulgasms sow the seeds that grow into your destiny."

Witold Andrew Ziarno

ACCELERATE 3-D MATERIALIZATIONS USING THE SOULGASM ENERGY METHOD.

In an ealier chapter we described the fact that emotions, what you feel about, charges or is the fuel behind rapid 3-D materializations. Once this fact is understood, You are at the point of using any activity that is pleasureable for You and creates a high vibration to fuel your materializations. The most powerful emotions are happiness, unconditional love, and sexual climax. They are super fuel. Ancient cultures have long used sexual energy in a variety of materialization practices. What was done involves the channeling of sexual energy to empower a desired materialization.

Energize your visualizations individually or with Your partner during sex (sacred energy exchange). Materializations are energized and accelerated with feeling and emotion during foreplay, intercourse, and thereafter. The stronger the emotion fueling the visualization/materialization, the faster the 3-D manifestation. Since sexual climax (and even more powerfully a Soulgasm described in a later chapter) is one of the strongest emotions humans experience in physical form, it is a powerful way to energize Your materializations. In the moment of climax, insert the thought and feeling of Your visualization (being there and here now), and call forth its rapid 3-D completion. Do this with your partner at the point of mutual climax to futher energize the visualization. The rest of You, the Universe, responds to this energy by an even "faster" alignment of all that is required for that materialization.

SEX (sacred energy exchange) rapidly accelerates 3-D materializations. There are many examples of self-healing using positive emotions e.g., laughter, euphoria. Applying the Soulgasm energy method to self-healing materializations speeds physical healing. The results are climactic to say the least. Similarly, it is well known that the right hand releases energy into the Universe and the left hand draws in energy from the Universe into your energy body and physical form. A particularly powerful method is at the point of climax to pull in the energy of the Universe into your physical and energy bodies and also to call forth the rapid alignment of all of Your Actions and the Actions of all those involved in your materializations. This method aligns process steps in a smoother process with fewer twists and turns. Ultimately, the Universe undersands how to organize All of the intricate details and actions of All players in the most efficient way. The energization of this process certainly does work, with results appearing fast and miraculously for each of the process steps for what appears to the mind to be complex 3-D materializations involving multiple players.

Chapter 10

"Trust the vibes you get, energy doesn't lie."

Scottie Waves

ACCELERATE THE 3-D MATERIALIZATIONS BY SHARING THEM ONLY WITH THOSE WHO ARE ALIGNED WITH YOUR MATERIALIZATIONS

Since We All are THE ONE SOUL, We All share the same power of creation. The only difference is how strongly we choose to use our power and in what direction we direct our energies. In your lifetime, You meet people who just click with You and align their actions and joy with your action and joy. These are what We call Soulfriends, be they in Your family or techinically outside of our biological families. On the flip side of the coin, You also meet people who have wishes that differ from Your wishes. Their wishes may be 180 degrees opposite of the wishes you desire to materialize. These are the people to observe, avoid, and disregard. Why? If You have one materialization, and someone has a nonaligned materialization e.g., one that is opposite your materialization, there is a plus and minus mathematical effect. This scenario is often observed in the family context. The child desires to go one route for their happiness in studies and other activities. The parent(s), who are under heavy control of their minds, desire that the child go in a different direction. Frequently, the child is directed into a career that is less than satisfying, one which they are less than passionate about all in an effort to be "practical" and satisfy the parents' wishes. This is a mistake, as there are nonaligned intentions going into the Universe, and involve a situation where those under the heavy influence of their minds (in this case the parents) desire a materialization that does not serve the best and highest good of the child's Soul and the child's Soul journey. In this scenario, it is best for the parents to observe what the child is passionate about, and provide the child freedom to materialize a career they are passionate about. The career that involves passion and service to others then also results in financial materializations that are satisfying due to the fact that the career has the right energy behind it.

A negative (minus) effect comes from the intention, doubt or fear energy of the other person. This energy may/may not effect how fast your 3-D materializations appears depending on how You safeguard Your materializations. To zero out the effect of those not aligned with your materialization for the best and highest good of all: 1) materialize a protective energy field in three ways; 2) call forth a bubble of white light protection energy around yourself and call forth a transmutation of the energy coming your direction to energy which supports your materialization; and 3) call forth another bubble around those sending out the negative energy neutralizing it, and transmuting it into positive energy. This method is powerful. It controls the energies headed your direction which have the purpose of slowing down your materializations or stopping them. Remember, those who are angry with you and that You wish to materialize have charged their wishes toward you with anger or envy energy. Anger and envy energies are very low vibrational energies that are easily transmuted into positive energies with Your higher vibrational energies of unconditional love, laughter, and joy. So pay no attention to the low vibers, while being observant of those whose intentions are not aligned with Your intentions. The low vibers are generating bad Karma for themselves. Another good technique is to keep your intentions and actions secret from lower vibing beings not aligned with Your wishes.

To power up Your wishes, share Your materializations with people who support them. There is a cummulative, synergistic effect of like-minded beings materializing the same positive end result. This further accelerates the 3-D process and is a very powerful Spiritual teamwork technique. Practically, the Miracle Makers assemble in a circle as has been described in many ancient writings and paintings, and use ritual white magic. All positive ritual white magic involves the casting of spells, which are nothing more than the directed intention, thoughts, feelings, words, and actions of the ritual makers toward a specific end result. Numerous treatises are available regarding positive ritual magic for focusing energies to end results. TYPICALLY, ALL RECITE AND FEEL THE MATERIALIZATION WITH YOU. ALL REPEAT THE VISION BOARD SPELL DAILY AS A TEAM, ALL ALREADY KNOWING IT IS DONE AT THE LEVEL OF CREATION. This is a fun way for All to share in individual and group materializations. As long as the ritual white magic includes the incantation as well as the feeling: "FOR THE BEST AND HIGHEST GOOD OF ALL, THE ONE SOUL, US ALL AND ALL CREATION," both the process and end result are Good. As described earlier, this is the ONLY way one should consider doing any of these practices because of the Karmic blowback effects described in a preceding chapter. To truly

BE a NATURAL BORN MIRACLE MAKER, practice White Magic. It is real. It is **GOOD.**

The author came across a brilliant effort made in Thailand which is sure to work miracles globally in the winter of 2016 which shows the world using the Spirit Team work materialization method. Over 1,000,000 children assembled in Thailand to meditate for world Peace. Why do they call Thailand the Land of Smiles? Many are at inner Peace. Their inner Peace then projects externally. Imagine events around the world in which hundreds of millions or billions of people join together simultaneously to meditate for world Peace as we move forward into the World Return to Paradise. The assembly and simultaneous use of Divine energies from All of these people ignites a shift of positive energy change across the globe of unprecendented scale and quickness. With the advent of social media platforms, organization of such large events is straightforward. Expect flashmobs of Peace. Materialize flashmobs of Peace. Peace materializes. So it is done.

Chapter 11

THE NUMBER AND SIZE OF YOUR MATERIALIZATIONS IS IRRELEVANT; YOUR VIBE AND WISH IS WHAT MATTERS.

As You are an infinite being masquerading in a limited physical human costume, there is zero limit on the number or size of your materializations. You may choose to materialize something small or large, a low cost item, high-end object, a small convenience as a parking spot in a full parking garage when and where you like it, a bottle of beer, small amounts of cash or large amounts of cash. How about materializing things on a really grand scale? Perhaps, a floating island chain, a new cinema studio, music festivals on monumental scales, world peace, an end to the militarization of the planet, a world free of borders and with minimal travel restrictions, new governmental models? Your same Divine energy goes into either materialization, small or large. All types of materializations come into three-dimensional reality. One hundred percent gauranteed, if You believe.

By way of example, the author and a consortium of large international partners are now materializing three floating islands called Return to Paradise Movie Islands which include 1.2 million square meters of space, are triangular, float by way of 28 meters of floating concrete, and are one kilometer on each side. The story around this materialization, which is in 3-D process now, involves miracles and synchrodestinies of epic proportions. In the fall of 2009, the author vision boarded with specificity (except for completion date at that time) a series of islands for the affluent. The vision board was created in the author's 200 square meter luxury home office in Odessa, Ukraine. In the winter of 2015, the author's master designer in California was requested to design the islands. He designed the islands as three tethered equilateral triangles with no input design by the author. Two months later, the author went on a business and personal trip to Kiev, Ukraine. Prior to his trip, the author booked a suite at the hotel Vissak in the Obolon region of Kiev not noticing the shape of the hotel on the booking website at all.

In Kiev, the author arrived at the Vissak hotel and had a couple of *Twilight Zone* moments. The first moment involved a look at the fire escape map of the hotel. It too was an equilateral triangle like the Return to Paradise movie islands. This was interesting but the synchrodestiny still did not completely register with the author. Then a producer from Ukraine's largest private film studio invited the author for a business meeting about 800 meters from the hotel Vissak. On his return to the hotel, the author walked by a second and third building identical to the hotel in shape. You may view the structures on Google Maps. The Universe had mirrored the three Return to Paradise Movie Islands in three huge buildings in Kiev constructed prior to the author's arrival there. Talk about destiny. Talk about Synchrodestiny. Synchronicity is the Universe saying yes to your Miracles, even to the largest physical materializations you can imagine. Synchronicity plus action is Synchrodestiny, Your fate. The mind may try to assert that this was a random event. Yet, there are zero random events in the lives of Us All, The One Soul. All events are synchronized by Natural Law. As such, choose to materialize the best, most interesting experiences, products, objects, relationships, etc. that you can imagine for the best and highest good of all. The Universe, THE ONE SOUL, cares not about the size, premium price or number of your materializations. You simply get what you specifically request. The Return to Paradise Movie Islands are completed by the end of 2020.

Another delicious story of materialization on a smaller scale is the author's materializations literally from the ether of beer, almost on command. One of the first such materializations occurred in Santa Margherita Ligurie, Italy on a warm summer night at the end of August 2015. A group of talented street musicians were playing The Rolling Stones' *I Can't Get No Satisfaction*. The author was super-charged with happiness, and since it was hot outside, he wished for a cold beer to enjoy. In no less than one minute, the author turned his head around and a new, unopened bottle of Heineken beer was one meter from the author on a ledge with no one to be seen around the beer. The author asked: "Who placed it there when there was no one around but the author who had no beer on him?" This was a clear "biracle." The author's thought materialized into a three-dimensional object from the ether. No more than three days from the writing of this chapter, the same type of "biracle" repeated itself. The author was in Nice, France on a summer day in July 2017 at the Côte d'Azure airport. Again, being a hot summer day, the author wished a cold beer and had a taste for Italian food. Within less than an hour, the author looks into his light baby blue travel bag, and there is a bottle of Heineken beer and a large plastic container of Italian pasta. The author does another wholely shit double take when these miracles occurred, but at this point the author remembers that he and All of You are Natural-born Miracle Makers, The Creator, and these miraculous events are daily occurrences at this point. All images of the miracles and biracles have been captured on the author's iPhone as evidence. The author is a technology lawyer by training and likes the cold, hard facts.

In addition to the miracles reported by this author, the author has also used the Law of Attraction/Creation to call forth like-minded Souls who are at very high vibrational levels. The Souls now appear every day, one by one, and the number is well into the several hundreds counting only from the beginning of 2017. Each report their own stories of materializations, and their thoughts becoming things. They speak of materializations of laptop computers that they wished, vacations, spouses, children, and many more delicious materializations. Many are users of the teachings laid out in *The Secret* film (Rhonda Byrne, 2006) which has a worldwide following, and it appears that the reports on Wikipedia are incorrect in terms of sales and penetration of the film and its teachings into the worldwide mass audience. The number of people who have seen and are using the film's teachings is well into the hundreds of millions.

There are several takeaway things to remember from this myriad of encounters and miracles: Those who think and feel cheap, get cheap experiences and products. Those who think and feel rich, get rich experiences and products. Again, THE ONE SOUL, YOU and THE REST OF YOU responds to how you think, feel, speak ABOUT YOUR SELF and act. YOU may wish to call this Your vibe. BE THE MULTI-MILLIONAIRE OR MULTI-BILLIONAIRE NOW WITH A WONDERFUL LUXURY LIFESTYLE EXPERIENCE NOW IN YOUR VISUALIZATIONS. IMAGINE BOTH GREAT THINGS TO BUILD, AND SMALL THINGS TO ENJOY. DO IT NOW. ADD AS MANY MATERIALIZATIONS AS YOU WISH TO YOUR VISION BOARD. Make Your vision board a vision wall in your apartment or house. YOU ARE AN INFINITE BEING AND CAN CREATE ALL YOU WISH NO MATTER WHO YOU ARE. KEEP THE VISION BOARD ORGANIZED. In this way you are delivered your wishes in an organized manner. Again, this is another example of THE NATURAL LAW OF MIRRORING. NOW YOU HAVE SET AND ENERGIZED YOUR INTENTIONS FOR THE MATERIALIZATIONS PROPERLY. THE UNIVERSE IS SET IN MOTION TO CREATE THE 3-D PROCESS EVENTS NECESSARY FOR THE MATERIALIZATIONS. BE ONE OF

THE GREATEST NATURAL-BORN MIRACLE MAKERS PLANET EARTH HAS EVER KNOWN. BE LEGENDARY. TAKE INSPIRED ACTION. I AM.

Chapter 12

"The Universe may cook up a dinner, but you have to feed yourself."
>Annie Zaleszak

LIGHTS, CAMERA, ACTION TIME FOR YOUR MATERIALIZATION(S).

IT IS TIME FOR YOU TO TAKE ACTION. Action is sometimes required for materializations. Some objects and experiences shall instantly appear for you to enjoy as described above. Others require action steps on your part as a part of the process of materialization. The Author has experienced both varieties of materializations, materializations requiring zero action (modern day miracles), some action, and extended action. Actions are of two types: 1) actions that the mind pushes, which may then be followed by doubt, fear, and inaction, and 2) actions that flow naturally with guidance from YOUR SOUL, THE ONE SOUL through messages, dreams, and synchronicities that illuminate your path. With respect to the type 1 actions the mind pushes, it is best to avoid these types of actions as they are generally not in harmony with THE ONE SOUL or with the infinite organizing power of THE ONE SOUL. By way of example, the author met Jan, a 26-year-old well-dressed Russian man, at a film festival in Vaduz, Liechtenstein. Jan worked as a driver for a wealthy Russian businessman and we chatted about the principles of materialization. Jan was familiar with The Law of Attraction principles. Jan wished to have his own business and not be a worker. Our conversation proceeded and in the next two weeks Jan was inspired with a new business idea. We assisted Jan gratis by filing a patent application with him on his new product concepts for his new business. The flow of ideas was exciting Jan, and he proceeded initially to start work on forming his new business with great enthusiam. Then his mind got active and he was questioning why the process was taking longer than his mind expected. Within a few weeks, we called Jan to check in with him and found out that he doubted he would be successful and stopped action on his business midstream. We advised Jan to continue, but he gave up. Jan engaged in mind activity outside the natural flow of the Universe in this example, and in essence self-sabotaged. Jan's example is one of the type of actions not to take that ends up in in-action. If you swim halfway across a river and stop, you drown. You must swim all the way to the other side. So it is with the action phase of the I AM materialization process.

The second type of action, THE ACTION OF THE ONE SOUL, YOU, flows naturally, and it is fun. This type of action is the realm of real magic. The real magic takes the form of guidance from the Universe and includes what appear to be chance encounters (yet the encounters are organized by the infinite organizing power of THE ONE SOUL). The real magic requires YOU to have an awareness of synchronicities and to take immediate action on the synchronicities as they are lighting Your path to your desired materialization, and to take instant action on the events that appear before You.

By way of example, the author is materializing a global series of large-scale Spiritual music festivals entitled Return to Paradise Music Festivals (produced by I AM MUZIK) featuring large international groups, nationally famous Artists for specific countries, and new talent. One group the author wished to materialize in the Ukraine for a festival in Odessa (2018, now) was Okean Elzy, one of the most famous bands in the Ukraine capable of filling football stadiums. The author properly vision boarded the band's participation in the festivals in the spring of 2017. The author then attended a music festival in Lviv, Ukraine, and set a meeting at a vegan restaurant one afternoon with a band that appears at the author's music festivals. As the author was walking to the restaurant, he turned to the left to ask a man for directions. We started talking shop. The man then told us that he is the tour manager for Okean Elzy. Magic. The Universe delivered. We instantly took action and exchanged contact information and then proceeded to do business. The author also wishes to mention that the Artist roster for the festivals has also filled up with amazing synchronous meetings with a variety of Spiritually attuned Artists. Their numbers have swelled the ranks of Festival(s) Artist rosters. The meetings happen two or three a day, with the author finding himself at the right place at the right time with Artists who have the right songs to perform, with the right vibe. In this way, the author has met Artists and their managers from the ranks of Internationally popular Popstars to Nationally famous Artists. The meetings have been pure magic. More to come.

Another example of how THE ONE SOUL organizes itself to guide you to the end result You wish to materialize occurred a week prior to the author writing this chapter. The author was in the airport in Nice heading back into Switzerland. Outside the airport the author strikes up a conversation with a gentleman from

Monaco returning from a trip to Thailand where the gentleman owns his own private island. The gentleman was on his way to his private apartment in St. Tropez, France, and a principle residence in Monaco. The gentleman revealed to the author that he owns a law firm, and has been involved in the film financing sector for the last 40 years. The author is materializing his own film studio with a portfolio of Spiritual themed films, **I AM STUDIO PRODUCTIONS**. We exhanged contact information and proceeded to organize subsqequent business actions to move film financing deals to completion. So you see, **THE ONE SOUL** rearranges itself in such a magical way that You meet all the people required for Your materialization to proceed to completion. The process is totally natural and dynamic, and requires You to have an awareness and openess to take action. You are completely guided by a loving **ONE SOUL**, through all of its different parts e.g., people, places, and things, so that the process is fun for all. As Jack Canfield teaches in *The Secret* film (Rhonda Byrne, 2006), getting to your destination is akin to driving a car from Chicago to California at night with the lights on. You see about seventy meters in front of You at any one time, yet that is enough to get You to Your final destination. Similarly, the Universe sets all that is required before You to get You to Your materializations every seventy meters at a time. Your job is to see the magical meetings, and take instant inspired action once the opportunities arise.

To have awareness of the synchronicities and actions required on Your end, have your third eye open. Your third eye is your pineal gland and many teachers throughout history have provided the techniques for opening your awareness, third eye, to see the synchronicities and guidance. In Ancient Egypt, the third eye was represented as the single Eye, and was known as the Seat of the Soul. Your third eye provides You with an awareness of the subtle and not so subtle guidance the rest of You, THE ONE SOUL, is providing to You to guide You to your final destination and materialization. The key is to have a de-calcified pineal gland so that You can see the magic as it is. "In the land of 20/20 vision, the third eyed woman/man is Queen and King." In short, All of Your experiences in Life are synchronized and guided. There are zero random events as we are All THE ONE SOUL, and THE ONE SOUL does organized, synchronized events between All parts of Itself.

By way of further example, look at the physical body Your Soul animates. It is an extension of You and was chosen by You to animate while Your Soul was still in the Spirit realm. Your body has billions upon billions of living cells. Within each cell, there are billions upon billions of molecules, each molecule knowing what to do and in which chemical reaction to engage in to keep You animated. All is perfectly synchronized in the dance of Life. The same holds true for the trillions of other living beings here on planet Earth all living together in ecosystems that dance to the harmony of the Universe. The action taken by each form of matter is synchronized one with another to create an experience. The only conclusion that can be drawn from this earthly dance is that **WE, THE CREATOR**, collectively in each individual form, are the **SUPREME INTELLIGENCE, BOTH IN DESIGN, FUNCTION AND ORGANIZATION. USE THIS SUPREME INTELLIGENCE WHEN TAKING ACTION ON YOUR MATERIALIZATIONS. IT IS THERE FOR YOU TO USE.**

YOUR JOB IS TO HAVE AN AWARENESS OF THE SYNCHRONICITIES IN LIFE GUIDING YOUR ACTIONS AND THE ACTIONS OF THOSE INVOLVED IN YOUR MATERIALIZATIONS. By way of further example, a delightful practice is a daily meditation asking **YOUR HIGHEST SELF** to introduce the synchronicities in Your life to guide You and all those involved in Your materializations, as well as to guide Your actions and the actions of the others in such a way that is fun, and for the best and highest good of All in the materialization process. The results You get are real guidance.

This author makes daily meditations at the start of the day requesting his HIGHEST SELF AND THE HIGHEST SELF OF ALL OTHERS INVOLVED in his materializations for the best and highest good of ALL for guidance. One such example also happened last week. The author asked for next steps in his materializations with respect to whom to visit and where to travel. The synchronicities that appeared on Instagram, Facebook, in what people were saying to the author were that the author should visit his longtime American attorney friend who resides in the Czech Republic with his wife and family. The author boarded a motorcoach and arrived at his friend's house, not having the friend's mobile phone contact details. Noticing no one was home, the author wondered if his friend went on a summer holiday. Within 10 minutes of the author's arrival, the friend's next-door neighbor arrived with his wife and called the friend's wife and the author was able to speak with his friend. The author's friend said he and his family are in Nice, France now for the summer. The author then spent two delicious days in Karlsbad, Czech Republic continuing to write this book on his iPhone in a local hotel as his intuition told him it was the thing to act on. Then the author proceeded with another morning meditation asking for next guidance steps. The synchronicities started flowing instantly after the meditation indicating that the author should proceed to Nice, France, which the author took instant action on. The synchronicities took the form of images appearing on Instagram, Facebook, in the French language speakers walking by the author in Karlsbad, Czech Republic, in the cars that were passing by the author with the license plate, 1961, the year the author's lawyer friend was born, and in other forms. THE ONE SOUL then organized the modes of transportation for the author as well as places to stay along the way there. The author was to be in Nice to meet the others who THE ONE SOUL organized there. All the guidance is harmonious for the best and highest good for all, and put in place to support the materializations.

After his stay in Nice, France, the author proceeded with another morning meditation requesting guidance for next steps, and the appearance of an Apple computer to continue writing this book, as the writing would be accelerated. The synchronicities indicated a return to Switzerland. So the author boarded a motorcoach from Nice to Zurich. The meditation included the request to meet new Spiritually aware friends and be able to continue to write this book on an iMac computer. The action the author took was to send a single Couchsurfing request to a fellow Couchsurfer, Achim, in Zurich, whom the author met two days before electronically on the

Couchsurfing website. Achim and the author immediately clicked and it turns out magically that Achim set his Apple computer in his guest bedbroom in his apartment on the Gold Coast of Lake Zurich two days before the author's arrival. Perfect synchrodestiny. The author then took action and kindly requested Achim if he had a computer he could use to write this book. Being the most gracious host, Achim responded yes. The guidance from THE ONE SOUL was perfect. A great new Spiritual friend appeared and an Apple computer appeared as called forth by the Author, and this book was completed.

ASKFORGUIDANCEFROMYOURHIGHEST SELF. THE GUIDANCE SYNCHRONICITIES APPEAR 100 PERCENT OF THE TIME. THE GUIDANCE SYNCHRONICITIES GUIDING YOUR ACTIONS TAKE MANY FORMS; WHAT SOMEONE AROUND YOU SAYS, OBJECTS ON YOUR PATH, LICENSE PLATES, NEW FB OR LINKEDIN CONTACT, LOCATIONS WHERE YOU FIND YOURSELF LIVING IN LIFE, ETC. We provide yet another business materialization example using synchronicity guidance. The author made a visualization in 2009 and 2010 to have companies based in Switzerland, and the ideas arrived for an earlier entrepreneurial venture (the LUMEDEN GROUP of medical device companies) and then later the author was inspired with the business ideas for the I

AM GROUPE of companies, including a cinema studio, music company, publishing house, property development company with floating islands, a coffee house chain, luxury fashion brands based on the film characters, and others. The author then chose to proceed with large-scale cash materializations including the materialization of 26 billion Swiss francs in abundance to enjoy and to share. The author observed very many impressive guidance synchrodestinies for all the materializations, and has recorded them all for the history books by I AM PUBLISHING HAUS AG (Newco). By way of further example, the author is materializing a collaboration with the world's largest cinema chain operator, Dalian Wanda Cinema, a subsidiary of the Dalian Wanda company in China owned by the Wang family, China's richest family. The syncrodestinies indicating the materializations were proceeding then took many forms. The author found himself living in Neu Wangs (New Wangs), Switzerland a couple of summers ago by happenstance. Then as the author returned to Ukraine in January 2017 and stayed at the Hotel Chernomorets in Kiev, he was given room number 26 as a synchrodestiny for the materialization, along with hundreds of repetitive appearances of the number 26 for this materialization. Similarly, Dr. Deepak Chopra in his book *Synchrodestiny* describes an event where he is flying over Lucerne, Switzerland

and is thinking about Dr. Carl Gustav Jung's book, *Synchronicity*. The author is basing the headquarters of the I AM GROUPE companies in Lucerne, Swizterland. Yet, another amazing synchrodestiny for the author's materializations. The guidance from THE ONE SOUL appears. The author continues with all inspired actions.

THE SYNCHRONICITY GUIDANCE TAKES ALL FORMS. WHEN THE SYNCHRONICITY APPEARS, TAKE ACTION ON IT IMMEDIATELY E.G., ACCEPT THE INVITATION, MAKE A CALL, SET UP A FACE TO FACE MEETING, GO TO THE PARTY, ETC. The synchronicities become synchrodestinies e.g., your fate when you follow their lead free of analysis by Your mind, and take action based on them instantly. This is the type of spontaneous joy-filled Life many call "being in the flow." All of Your actions are based on the guidance of THE ONE SOUL, YOU. Time stands still and You are just happy doing the action.

Chapter 13

"Your thoughts, your tongue, and your actions must ALL be painting the same picture."

Joe Vitale

ALIGN ALL OF YOUR THOUGHTS, FEELINGS, WORDS, AND ACTIONS WITH YOUR MATERIALIZATION(S).

THE ONE SOUL, the rest of You mirrors back to You your thoughts, feelings, words, and actions e.g., the sum total of who You believe You are. All must be aligned to materialize properly and quickly. In particular, the actions You take must be consistent with Your materializations. Why? If all is unaligned, there is a mathematical plus minus effect that retards Your materializations. As such, Your thoughts, feelings, words, and what you do must be in alignment (not canceling each other out) during the materialization process. In other words, do not wish a millionaire lifestyle and go, as an action, to buy cheap shoes. This wish is misaligned with action, and is a mistake. By way of example, the author materialized a beautiful pair of Fellini Italian leather dress shoes on his journey in Kiev. The author did not look at the price of the shoes or the amount of cash he had in his pocket. The author did not have enough cash to purchase the shoes at the time he entered the Fellini store in Kiev, but knowing how materialization works, the author took action, tried the shoes on, felt he already was enjoying them, and then asked the shop attendant to place them on the side so he could return to purchase them later. The author's actions, thoughts, feelings, and words were aligned for the materialization. He liked the shoes, and then materialized the cash necessary for the shoes within two hours of setting them aside for purchase. The author then continued his travels in Europe, and enjoys walking as part of his fitness routine. Walking is a wonderful way to experience life and be able to notice synchronicities and just take time to BE. The author then walked several thousand kilometers in his Fellini Italian shoes until the soles wore through.

Time for new dress shoes, and the visualization was made. The author found himself in the delightful city of Bern, Switzerland to pick up his new 10-year European passport at an embassy there. While in Bern, the author noticed that there were super summer sales going on, and noticed a high quality pair of Swiss made black leather dress shoes were in a small shop with a pleasant English speaking owner. The author tried the pair on and it turned out that the 400 Swiss franc shoes were on sale for 50 Swiss francs. The Universe put the author in the right place at the right time for the materialization of the new dress shoes to replace the old pair. The author didn't have the 50 Swiss francs on him at the time, but went through the aligned action process and requested the cinema loving shop owner to set the dress shoes aside telling him that he would return the next day to purchase the dress shoes. The author then materialized the 50 Swiss francs necessary for the dress shoes, and the next day purchased them for his continuing travels.

All of these real examples illustrate that when Your thoughts, feelings, words, and actions are all aligned, The ONE SOUL, the rest of YOU, always synchronistically re-aligns itself for Your materialization one hundred percent of the time. Moments ago, the author stepped outside on the balcony to enjoy a pipe smoke. The Universe instantly delivered two more synchrodestinies for the materialization of the white Maserati GranCabrio present for the author's beloved as a white Audi Cabriolet pulled up below the balcony instantly followed by a white

VW Cabrio. We have written about this materialization in an earlier chapter and THE ONE SOUL is giving synchronistic guidance that the materialization is proceeding to 3-D form at the perfect time. THE MORALS OF THESE REAL LIFE STORIES ARE TO ALIGN ALL YOUR ACTIONS NOW: GO TO THE LUXURY CAR OR YACHT DEALER, ORDER THE LUXURY CAR OR YACHT. AND TAKE THE TEST DRIVE NOW. DO THE ALIGNED ACTIONS TO FEEL THE LUXURY CAR OR YACHT IS ALREADY YOURS, FULLY PAID FOR OR LEASED. SIGN THE CONTRACT, WRITE THE BOOK OR SCREENPLAY SO YOUR ACTIONS ARE ALIGNED WITH THE END RESULT THAT IS YOUR MATERIALIZATION.

The process of creation is perfectly efficient and your aligned actions are guided. The guidance may involve a nonlinear process. The limited ego thinks linearly as in assembling a puzzle e.g., border first, then interior. YOUR SOUL, THE CREATOR, THE ONE SOUL knows no such linear limitation. YOUR SOUL, THE ONE SOUL assembles "the puzzle image" that is your materialization by putting in All puzzle pieces in the most perfectly timed way as long as You are in complete alignment to receive that which You wish to materialize. This is called the flow of the Universe. YOUR JOB IS TO FOLLOW THE FLOW OF THE UNIVERSE ON ALL ACTION

ITEMS, INCLUDING TWISTS AND TURNS INVOLVED IN ALL MATERIALIZATIONS. THE MATERIALIZATION PROCESS IS DYNAMIC. BE FLEXIBLE AS THE PLAYERS INVOLVED IN THE MATERIALIZATIONS MAY CHANGE AS THE UNIVERSE ORGANIZES THE BEST AND HIGHEST GOOD FOR EACH SOUL. On business materializations as well as personal materializations, the players may change with THE ONE SOUL putting each person in place or removing them in the most perfectly timed, dynamic manner. YOU, THE ONE SOUL, IS DYNAMIC AND IN CONSTANT MOTION WITH RESPECT TO YOUR MATERIALIZATION. The limited mind may think that there is one or a handful of ways to Your end result. This is a mistake. YOU, THE CREATOR, THE ONE SOUL has an infinite number of creative ways to get to the end result that is Your materialization. BE PEACEFUL AND COMFORTABLE AT EACH DYNAMIC TWIST AND TURN, WHILE KEEPING YOUR FOCUS ON THE END RESULT.

Chapter 14

"Everything you desire is coming. Relax and let the universe pick the timing and the way. You just have to trust that what you wish is coming, and watch how fast it comes."

Abraham Hicks

THE "TIMING" OF YOUR MATERIALIZATIONS IS ALWAYS PERFECT; TRUST THE PROCESS.

REMEMBER THAT YOUR SOUL, THE ONE SOUL, LIVES IN THE REAL PRESENT MOMENT, AND THAT IN THIS PRESENT MOMENT THE TIMING OF YOUR MATERIALIZATIONS IS ALWAYS AS IT SHOULD BE. IT IS PERFECT AND OPTIMIZED. The limited mind/ego lives in the grand illusion of "time." As such, it impatiently asks: "When are my goodies going to arrive?" and the limited mind/ego may try to derail the materialization process it it takes "too long" for it to see the goodies unless it is the perfect servant of Your Soul. The mind/ego becomes the perfect servant of YOUR SOUL when it serves its purpose. Its purpose being to use logic when logic is called for in any individual process step. That is it. The purpose of the mind/ego is other than questioning when a materialization should appear in the illusion of "time." The mind's job is practical, executing action steps logically when they appear.

The Spiritual Master knows that the timing of materializations is always optimized, and keeps her/his mind from asking the "timing of delivery" question knowing that the question only causes doubt and suffering for the person asking the question. IN SHORT, THE TIMING OF YOUR MATERIALIZATION IS ALWAYS PERFECT SO DISREGARD THE ILLUSION OF "TIME" FACTOR AND GO HARMONIOUSLY WITH THE FLOW OF UNIVERSAL ENERGIES AS EACH STEP OF YOUR PROCESS UNFOLDS FOR YOUR PARTICULAR MATERIALIZATION. CELEBRATE ALL SUCCESSES, LARGE AND SMALL, ON YOUR MATERIALIZATION PATH. Organize parties with your high vibing aligned friends to celebrate successes related to each action item you complete along your materialization path.

YOUR MIND MAY BE ASKING WHY IT IS RELEGATED TO THE JOB OF EXECUTING

PROCESS STEPS ONLY? WELL, THAT IS ITS PURPOSE; TO BE THE SERVANT OF YOUR SOUL, SERVICING THAT WHICH REQUIRES EXECUTION. YOU, YOUR SOUL, ALREADY ARE THE END RESULT, AND ITS ENTIRE CREATION PROCESS AND ALL ACTION STEPS THEREIN INCLUDING THE "TIMING" OF THE ULTIMATE 3-D MATERIALIZATION OF YOUR WISH. YOU, THE CREATOR, THE ONE SOUL HAS ORGANIZED THE PROCESS TO BE FUN FOR ALL. Your mind is the pair of hands (mind-hands) that executes three-dimensional orders. Your mind-hands work the lump of clay that becomes the final beautifully crafted vase in a fun way. The more fun You feel at each action step using your mind-hands in their proper role, as a servant, BY THE LAW OF CREATION/ATTRACTION, THE MORE FUN THE REST OF YOU, THE ONE SOUL, DELIVERS TO YOU.

Chapter 15

"Appreciation is the highest form of prayer, for it acknowledges the presence of good wherever you shine the light of your thankful thoughts."

Alan Cohen

USING THE LAW OF APPRECIATION/ GRATITUDE TO ACCELERATE YOUR MATERIALIZATION MIRACLES.

Forget "praying." Prayer is a lie. Prayer means that you do not have something You wishing and praying for something sends the signal of lack into the Universe. Praying is a mistake. Instead, when you rise in the morning express appreciation for all the goodness that surrounds you. Throughout the day express appreciation for all that You enjoy. When you fall asleep at night express appreciation for all the little and big miracles you have experienced throughout your day. Express appreciation for your health, wealth, family, and friends. **EXPRESS GRATITUDE AT EACH**

PROCESS STEP YOU ARE ENGAGED IN FOR YOUR MATERIALIZATIONS, INDIVIDUALLY AND WITH YOUR SOUL FAMILY. Why? Gratitude or thankfulness is a strong emotion meaning "I like what I am experiencing." The more grateful You are for All the Good things You are experiencing, the more of it is mirrored back to You by THE ONE SOUL, THE REST OF YOU. Lack of appreciation for All good things You are experiencing or praying for materializations has the effect of turning the faucet off for more good things and is a huge mistake. Avoid ungratefulness and prayer completely. Gratitude also accelerates the transformation of Your intention into three-dimensional form. The author practices expressing gratitude continually every moment. When smoking his pipe, when walking in an aromatic forest. Everywhere. All the "time." Introduce this practice in Your daily life, and watch that which You are grateful for multiply a thousandfold.

Chapter 16

"The more we share, the more we have."
Leonard Nimoy

THAT WHICH YOU DO FOR/TO THE OTHER, YOU DO TO/FOR YOURSELF: SHARE MATERIALIZATIONS AND ABUNDANCE.

As You remember who You are, THE CREATOR, in more and more present moments, and as You remember how to be Adept in materializing, the more You are drawn to share with All around You. There are several main reasons why You choose to share more: 1) You materialize more abundance; 2) You remember You are an unlimited being and can materialize even more than You shared; 3) You remember that "the other" You are sharing with is actually You in another costume; 4) Your signal to the Universe, the rest of You, is that You have the abundance to share, so more and more abundance is mirrored back to You; and 5) That there is zero scarcity of anything. More is simply materialized in any situation.

RELISH IN THE JOY OF SHARING THE MATERIALIZATIONS AND WISDOM OF HOW YOU CREATED THEM WITH OTHERS, AND CALL FORTH NEW, EVEN LARGER MATERIALIZATIONS USING WHAT YOU HAVE MATERIALIZED AS A STEPPING STONE FOR GREATER AND GREATER MATERIALIZATIONS.

Chapter 17

"The mind is a wonderful servant, but a terrible master."

Robin Sharma

THE TIMING OF YOUR MATERIALIZATIONS; PART II, HOW TO CAGE AN OVERACTIVE MIND/EGO.

Many of You are now Adept at the various process steps described in Natural-born Miracle Makers. Now, those of You whose minds are still active to a certain extent may be asking about the timing of Your manifesations. "Why is it taking so long?" Your ego may ask. Everyone with an uncaged ego asks this question. The question may come from Your mind/ego or the mind/ego of another. When a being with an active/overactive ego asks this question, be aware of who is talking to You. It is not their SOUL, YOUR SOUL, asking the question, but rather a mask/ego over THE SOUL doing the questioning. Similarly, if Your mind is asking the question, remember that You are not the thoughts being generated by Your mind/ego. YOU ARE YOUR SOUL. YOU ARE A SPIRIT HAVING A TEMPORARY physical human experience animating Your physical body. You also have a mind/ego in this incarnation. Your mind/ego is also not who You really are. YOU ARE YOUR SOUL. You may also wish to consider Your mind/ego and that of the other people around You as a "mask." The "mask/ego" covers up who you really are YOUR SOUL, THE ONE SOUL, THE CREATOR. Once You have an awareness of who is speaking NOW, Your mask/ego or that of another, and the thoughts and speech it is generating, You are in the perfect position to look at the thought, remember it is not you, and put it down on the table if You will, and choose another thought to think or entertain.

THE "MASK"/EGO IS THE ONLY REASON PEOPLE FAIL AT BEING NATURAL-BORN MIRACLE MAKERS AND FAIL IN THE MATERIALIZATION PROCESS. In terms of others' masks/egos, and your own mask/ego, ask which type of being is this thought coming from. Only three types of physical beings exist for You to meet and materialize with on earth. Type 1: The mindfools/the mask wearers. These are beings who wear a mask, and have completely forgotten they are THE CREATOR. Their minds or the minds of others have fooled the mindfools into forgetting who they really are. Behind their masks IS US, THE ONE SOUL, UNCONDITIONAL LOVE. The mask fears and doubts and fails to create or has a slow linear creation process or materializes only for the sake of their ego. The mask lives only in the illusion of time. Type 2: Bipolar. These are beings that oscillate between the poles of being a mindfool/mask wearer, and living FROM THIER SOUL, THE ONE SOUL, UNCONDITIONAL LOVE. These beings may be ineffective MIRACLE MAKERS since they go back and forth between creating and negating their creations with fear, doubt, and lack of action. Type 3: GODDESSES/GODS ON EARTH. THOSE WHO REMEMBER THEY ARE THE CREATOR. These are beings that live entirely AS THE ONE SOUL, UNCONDITIONAL LOVE IN HUMAN FORM IN EVERY MOMENT. THESE BEINGS ARE GOD WALKING IN a human costume sans the mask of the ego ALL THE TIME. THESE BEINGS ARE THE MOST POWERFUL MATERIALIZERS BECAUSE THEY REMEMBER THEY ARE THE CREATOR.

So when you look at the source of the thought when asked about the timing of your materializations, does the question come from a Type 1 or Type 2 being. If so, be aware of it, and BE free to completely disregard it. Type 3 beings do not ask the question because they remember who You are and who they are. These people are

Your materialization tribe. YOU RECOGNIZE THESE TYPE 3 PEOPLE BY THEIR VIBE. THEY ARE WHAT THE TRUE RELIGIONS HAVE CALLED SAINTS, PROPHETS, BUDDHAS, KRISHNAS, MESSIAHS, GODDESSES, GODS, ETC. THESE ARE THE INSTANT MIRACLE MAKERS WHOSE THOUGHTS CREATE MATTER FROM THE ETHER.

Advanced Miracle Makers use one of three processes to materialize. Process One. Thought instantly materializes into a 3-D object or experience. This Author has documented many such real life examples in his life which appear in the film that accompanies this book, and are also described herein. This is instant manifestation, a biblical level miracle e.g., resurrection, turning water into wine, miracle of the fish and loaves of bread, biracles, cash materializations e.g., Jesus Christ and other miracle maker level types of experiences. Process Two. Thought materializes quickly into 3-D object or experience with short "time" delay. The time delay in Process Two is a process that is designed perfectly as described above. First, here on earth, the three-dimensional world, there is a time delay introduced by the YOUNIVERSE to serve you. Process Three. Depending on your wish/intention, it is possible that your wish involves a series of process steps which require "time" to be put in place in a fun and enjoyable way for all players involved in the process. Where the process of creation flows from Your Soul, THE ONE SOUL, and You revel in the process itself, it is called inspired Art (IN SPIRIT ART). These are universally recognized by all Souls here as Masterpieces of Art, Literature, Music, Dance, Invention, etc. Inspired (IN SPIRIT) Action has been designed into the process by the Youniverse as part of the Fun of the Process of Creation here on earth. Think of an Artist wishing to create a beautiful vase from clay. There is a lump of clay on her potter wheel. If she simply wished the beautiful vase to appear, she would not enjoy the pleasure of fashioning the lump of clay with her hands on the potter's wheel, adding each curve to the final creation, hardening the clay in the furnace, and painting the vase with her final designs. So you see, action and "time" required is designed into the process of creation here on earth for our enjoyment and pleasure.

Here is how things work from an operational perspective in Processes Two and Three above: First, remember we are ALL THE ONE SOUL, HENCE WE ARE ALL CONNECTED. Your thought/wish from Your localized consciousness goes into COLLECTIVE CONSCIOUSNESS of WHICH WE ALL ARE A PART, THE ONE SOUL. From there another localized consciousness (person, animal, or object) picks up Your thought and in response thereto does an action e.g., appears, performs some action (leaves a new, cold, full bottle of Heineken for You to enjoy on a hot Italian evening), WHATEVER. Think of All of Us as a very large Internet with information flowing from a first node through a vast connected network to one or more other nodes who then act on the information to obtain the result desired by the first node. This is how materializations work from a rational perspective.

Chapter 18

"Self-sabotage is when we say we wish something and then go about making sure it doesn't happen."
Alyce P. Cornyn-Selby

HOW THE mindfools/mask wearers SELF-SABOTAGE OR SABOTAGE THEIR MATERIALIZATIONS; THE SOLUTION IS TO BE A TYPE 3 BEING, ALLONE.

The mind/mask/ego is only your friend when it is YOUR SOUL'S LOYAL SERVANT. There are three ways a mindfool's materializations are self-sabotaged by the mind/ego/mask. 1) Lack of Action. What happens if you fail to take action to realize your Intention? The result is that you self-sabotage. The result is that there is no result, no three-dimensional manifestation. 2) Doubt; and 3) Fear. Doubt and Fear kill what You wish about. There are the tools of what this author calls "The Old World Order." They mindfool humanity into doubting that they are

THE CREATOR. They create an atomosphere of fear to push their world control agenda through and to make a profit. They push fear as a tool to separate people and cause conflicts, wars, etc. In this case, the mindfools use doubt and fear to cause their audience to choose another materialization: the opposite of the original wish. Once you remember these tactics, You are in a position to ensure they have zero bearing on Your materializations. The root cause of All unfulfilled materializations is forgetting You are **THE CREATOR** and permitting Your monkey mind/mask/ego or the monkey mind/mask/ego of another to overanalyze, doubt, fear, and cause your body to stop actions to take You to the end result which is Your materialization.

The Natural-born Miracle Makers who materialize quickly remember they are ALLONE. Being ALLONE means to BE whole and complete within Your Self. Natural-born Miracle Makers are independent, free from the mindfoolery of the mind/ego/mask, either their own or that of others. The way to **BE ALLONE** is to find time away from other distractions in nature or in a quiet room as the Divine being You already are sans mind/ego/mask in meditation. All meditation is turning off the thought process, and just being. When you meditate, You put yourself into a state of stillness and silence. Meditation opens Your Self up to inner guidance and generates opportunities as profound ideas come to You that are useful for both your daily life and long-term success. When You meditate, love Your Self into a deep space of Unconditional Love, your partner, your family, and All creation. From this State of being, You open the doors to the power of creation itself to flow through you, the conduit. Meditation also gives You the energy to take Action continuously, and brings you into a state of being ALLONE. Meditation quiets the workings of the mind. Meditation makes the mind the servant of Your Soul. Meditation puts Your mind in its proper place for its proper function. The key is not to be mind-less, but to use your mind for its intended purpose; logic, when logic is required to implement a materialization which is created at the level of **THE SOUL. BEING ALLONE, YOU WORK MIRACLES** with your mind being **YOUR SOUL'S LOYAL SERVANT.**

Chapter 19

"When I was five years old, my mom told me that happiness is the key to life. When I went to school, they asked what I wanted to be when I grew up, I wrote down "happy." They told me I did not understand the assignment and I told them they didn't understand life."

John Lennon

WHY MANIFEST/MATERIALIZE? ANSWER: FOR ADDITIONAL HAPPY EXPERIENCES, TO AUGMENT THE HAPPINESS THAT IS ALREADY YOU.

Why do or should You manifest? You manifest experiences here on earth for one simple reason. To enjoy additional enjoyment in the physical experience of Life. REMEMBER: YOU ALREADY ARE HAPPINESS WITHIN, WITH OR WITHOUT OUTER OBJECTS AND EXTERNAL EXPERIENCES. Outer experiences or objects make you no more than temporarily happy or sad, at best. Those who require objects or experiences from the outside of themselves for happiness are never truly happy. An object itself (money, fur, luxury car, vacation) does not create happiness in and of itself. Your happiness comes from within You and is already there. Objects and relationships are for You to enjoy while Happiness emanates from within You. In the manifestation/materialization process, the most important step to accelerate the process of three-dimensional manifestation is to BE HAPPY NOW as described in earlier chapters. This is the emotional fuel that drives the creation of the three-dimensional object or experience e.g., health, wealth, etc. This is why all the Spiritual Masters throughout history have taught two things: Believe your wish/intention is already done. BE HAPPY NOW and in the experience you desire.

Chapter 20

"I do feel a connection to the divine and to the infinite."

> Joan Osborne, Artist,
> *What if God is One of Us*

WHO AM I? PART II. YOU ARE THE ABSOLUTE, SO WORK MIRACLES FROM YOUR NATURAL STATE AND EXPERIENCE WHO YOU ARE.

Dr. Deepak Chopra correctly teaches that The Absolute, The Creator, All of Us in human and other form, is the Field of All Possibilities. Any thing is possible. When we, each individually, make an intention or wish, we choose a possibility out of this infinite field to enjoy an experience, a feeling e.g., Happiness, Love, Excitement, etc. The entire Universe, **THE REST OF US, THE ONE SOUL**, then rearranges itself to create this 3-D experience for us and the feeling. Selecting a possibility from **THE FIELD OF ALL POSSIBILITIES** involves You already believing that it is done, and feeling the emotions related to the experience. In this way, You have locked in that possibility to experience. Since we are the Creator, the experience is guarenteed to be delivered. Now the cool three for one bonus the Universe delivers is this: When You make the wish, You already are super-charged with Happiness. Bonus One. When You go through the Action steps of molding the experience, you are further super-charged with Happiness. Bonus Two. When the object manifests, you enjoy a third charge of Happiness with the materialization. Bonus Three.

There is zero substitute for experiencing You are The Creator here on earth. You can read about miracles worked by others, including this author, remembering that they are the Creator e.g., The Author's, Jesus', The Apostles', Mose's, and other's miracles. The IAMG (I AM GOD) moment is when You, Your Self remembers/self-realizes You actually are the Creator through the experience of Creation and the working of Miracles. Coinciding with Your IAMG moment is always a HUGE dose of Happiness. Super design by the Youniverse for our experiences here on earth.

Chapter 21

"You and I are essentially infinite choice-makers. In every moment of our existence, we are in that field of all possibilities where we have access to an infinity of choices."

Deepak Chopra

WHAT MIRACLES MAY YOU MATERIALIZE/MANIFEST? PART II; BE THE DIVINE POWER YOU ALREADY ARE.

What Miracles can You manifest/materialize? The Answer is simple and grand at the same time. Anything. Any experience You wish. Yes, it's true, You can manifest anything. A new house. A new car. A loving family. Super orgasmic sex. Lots of cool friends. Huge financial abundance. A fulfilling career. The best grades at school and university. Jewelry. New designer clothes. Cash. A super-successful business. Perfect health. A slim body. A muscular body. A pizza. Happy days. You name it. You can manifest it. You are all the Creator in Human form. All that you see around You is You. You choose to come here on earth in 3-D form to create experiences for Yourself to BE HAPPY, as though You were on an extended vacation in 3-D form. There are zero limits on what You can materialize. This is Your Super Power.

Your only true power for working miracles resides within Your Self. It involves remembering that You are THE CREATOR, THE ONE SOUL, UNCONDITIONAL LOVE, and that ALL AROUND YOU IS SIMPLY YOU IN ANOTHER FORM. Looking outside of Your Self for any reason to other forms only serves to diminish the power and perfection within You already. The outside can only match Your "interior" perfection, or be less than Your powerful perfection already inside You. The exterior is never more than You, for it is You. If your mind/mask/ego or the mind/mask/ego of another tells You that You are less than the Creator, and cannot materialize something, and You believe them, You Both are wrong.

Here is another example of a delightful materialization completed by the author. You materialize all that You wish. By way of example, the author was in Cannes, France during the 68th Cannes Film Festival, and made an early morning meditation calling forth interviews with the international press to share the pipeline of the new films that were in pre-production at his new film studio and get general press coverage. Then the author simply went onto the walkway and sat in one of the rows of ocean blue chairs near the yacht moorings for enjoying the view of the marina. Within an hour of the meditation and request, Matthew Stock, a Reuter's reporter and his cameraman from London, approached the author and requested an interview. The interview was published online, and Matthew Stock wrote: "The stage is nearly set for the 12-day pageant described by film industry insiders like Andrea Ziarno as 'the place to be.' The day was followed by seven other international press interviews from press in Germany, Japan, Italy, The Netherlands, and a few other countries. The Universe delivered the called forth result very, very quickly.

Another major example follows: the author, NOW BEING AT ONE WITH ALL CREATION, continuously regularly performs weather miracles on a biblical scale on demand. This involves use of the I AM principle and results in the Sun coming out, clouds dissipating, or it starting to rain as required. The author has documented hundreds of weather miracles where the weather changes as the author calls forth within a matter of minutes or hours. While living in St. Gallen, Switzerland, and Lutsk, Ukraine, the author regularly performed such miracles and documented the results with his iPhone. The process is really nothing new as many such miracles have been reported in the Old and New Testaments, and all indigenous people are aware of these abilities which are invoked by "Rainmen" and "Shamans" in many indigenous cultures. You too have the same abilities and powers if You choose to exercise them. Just do it. You are thunderously suprised, or enjoy a sunny day, on demand. The reason these weather miracles work is that the elements are simply another form of us, the clouds, the rain, the Sun, the wind, etc. Being part of US ALL, THE ONE SOUL, in physical form, we can direct their movement and function.

Chapter 22

"Synchronicity is an ever-present reality for those who have eyes to see it."
Dr. Carl Gustav Jung

"Believing as I do in the theory of reincarnation, I live in the hope that if not in this birth, in some other birth I shall be able to hug all of humanity in friendly embrace."
Mahatma Gandhi

SYNCHRONICITY AND REINCARNATION; LAWS OF NATURE AND FACTS OF LIFE.

What are Synchroniticities? They are messages from THE ONE SOUL, THE OTHER PARTS OF YOU, animate and inanimate, in all forms of communication, that you are on track for your manifestations/materializations of Happiness, and are in the Action phase of manifestation/materialization. Synchronicity is the Universe saying "Yes" to You that Your materializations are already done at the level of creation, and are now being mirrored back to You in three-dimensional form. As described above, Synchronicities also serve as guidance for You on which action steps to take next for your materializations. In this way, The Universe delivers more fun for You as the 3-D realization process moves forward. Synchronicity is a Law of Nature, in the same way that Gravity is a Law of Nature. All Natural Laws work together harmoniously, including the Natural Laws of Synchronicity and Reincarnation.

Dr. Carl Jung coined the term in his work "Synchronicity." This author has captured hundreds of thousands of truly amazing synchronicities associated with the author's manifestations/materializations with his smartphone. Synchronicities appear before us everyday for those who choose to see them. By way of further example, the author is aware of truly impressive synchronicities associated with the reincarnation of the author's mother, reincarnated as a beautiful young woman in the city of Donetsk, Ukraine, Ludmila P. (known as the film character, Lucie Merci, in the quadrilogy of feature films premiering from I AM STUDIO PRODUCTIONS AG (Newco) shortly), who associated with the author's new companies and their principal business location in Switzerland, and cinema business partners in China, The Dalian Wanda Cinema Group. The country telephone code for

Switzerland is +41, and the country telephone code for China is +86. 1941 is the year of birth of the author's mother and 1986 is the year of death of the author's mother. The author has also collected hundreds of thousands of data points and used the Nature Law of Synchronicity as evidence to validate the Natural Law of Reincarnation, and his mother's reincarnation. The story of how the author determined that the beautiful young woman Ludmila P. was the reincarnation of his mother is truly amazing.

In the fall of 1986, about two months before the author's mother died from breast cancer at The University of Chicago Hospital, the author had a dream. As Dr. Carl Gustav Jung properly notes: "We have forgotten the age-old fact that God speaks chiefly through dreams and visions." The dream involved a beautiful young woman with long flowing hair riding a stunning white horse and wearing a red dress. The author felt that the beautiful young woman possessed his mother's Soul, but her physical form was new. The author shared the dream with his family, and on 6 12 (December), 1986, the author's mother Czeslawa Ziarno passed away. The next synchronicities followed. She died in hospital room number 612 at The University of Chicago Hospital. The recurring synchronicities were the numbers 612. The author was raised as a Roman Catholic and did not focus on reincarnation at the time, mistakenly thinking that we all only had one life here on earth. Decades passed and the author by fate found himself in the Ukraine for a reason. All events and the places we find ourselves are perfectly organized by THE ONE SOUL, for our individual and collective Soul journey of self-discovery and self-realization. In 2013, the author met Ludmila P. on an internet dating site called Mamba.ru. Ludmila and the author engaged in a chat and phone call exchange over a period of weeks, and chose to meet in person in Dnipropetrovsk, Ukraine at the Bartolomeo resort. Outside our hotel room in the garden was again the synchronicity: a statue of a white horse. The author and Ludmila P. continued with a romantic relationship for several months in Kiev during their last revolution, and the author then found himself in Odessa, Ukraine, living at the hotel Ekaterina with his white Great Dane, Sultan. Ludmila P. was invited to visit the author, and he suggested a photosession as Ludmila P. was studying model management at a University in Kiev and was herself a model. Ludmila P. organized the makeup artist and photographer, and suggested that we do the photoshoot at the beach on a white horse. The flash of rememberance moment happened. Then the author remembered the white horse dream, its meaning, and the fact that Ludmila P. looked exactly like the girl in the dream.

Sometime later, the author shared with Ludmila P. that she is the reincarnation of his mother. Ludmila P. did not believe the author at that time and Ludmila P. left the romantic relationship with the author. The author then found himself living and working on his businesses in Arbon, Switzerland. Further, amazing synchronicities appeared there illustrating that Ludmila P. was the reincarnation of Czeslawa Ziarno, the author's mother (protrayed in the films as Charlotte Obolon). The building at Rathausgasse 1, Arbon, Switzerland where the author lived and worked in the fall of 2014 and the spring of 2015 was built in the year 1260, again the December 6th synchronicity pointing to the reincarnation. There is a plaque on the building indicating that it was renovated in 1941, the year the author's mother was born. Again, the synchrodestiny. The author continued to try to reconnect with Ludmila P. Then the author took a trip to try to meet with Ludmila P. in Kiev. The author went to the Obolon region in Kiev where she lived and to the GPS location where Ludmila was posting Instagram photos on the Obolonska Naberezhna street along the Dnieper River. At the exact GPS location where Ludmila P. was posting some of her Instagram photos, was a white van next to a red Kia Picanto (Polish flag and Swiss flag colors synchronicity) with the license plate, 1986, the exact year that

Czeslawa Ziarno passed away. The author then proceeded to capture and archive thousands of other syncrhonicities confirming that Ludmila P. was the reincarnation of his mother, Czeslawa Ziarno, as well as many other synchronicities concerning her other previous incarnations, and the author's and others previous incarnations for those in the author's Soul family. The previous incarnations are significant historical incarnations.

Based on this evidence, We have called forth and materialize more than one Nobel Prize on the Natural Laws of Synchronicity, Synchrodestiny, and Reincarnation. Why you may ask are the synchronicities appearing? Answer: It is THE ENTIRE ONE SOUL confirming that it has re-arranged itself to Manifest that which You have called Forth, and confirming Natural Laws for all of humanity to understand. There are zero random events in Life. All events happen for a reason. Synchronicities are loads of fun. Enjoy them. Laugh when they appear. They are harbingers for Your 3-D Materializations. The Universe is truly amazing and has choreographed the dance of synchronicities for your pleasure, and to help us remember who we all are, and who we were.

Chapter 23

> "Happiness comes to those who appreciate what they have already."
>
> The Buddha

THE ROLE OF HAPPINESS IN THE UNIVERSAL LAW OF ATTRACTION/ CREATION AS APPLIED TO WORKING MIRACLES AS A NATURAL-BORN MIRACLE MAKER.

When You ARE HAPPINESS NOW, during each and every stage of the I AM (Intention Action Manifestation) process, You experience even more Happiness. This is what has been called the Law of Attraction in popular circles. You attract to You more of that which You believe You are already or are experiencing already. You and the entire Youniverse, THE ONE SOUL, are delivering the experience of Happiness in rapid-fire mode. You are attracting Happy people into Your Life, Happy events, Happy synchronistic meetings, anything that is required to advance Your Ultimate Manifestation of Happiness.

Chapter 24

"The ego is only an illusion, but a very influential one. Letting the ego-illusion become your identity can prevent you from knowing your true self. Ego, the false idea of believing that you are what you have or what you do, is a backwards way of assessing and living life."

Dr. Wayne Dyer

NATURAL-BORN MIRACLE MAKERS
OPERATE AS THE SELF sans ego
AND EFFORTLESSLY ENTER ALL
ENCOUNTERS WITH OTHERS.

The ego desires its own Happiness without regard for the Happiness of the rest of the SELF, THE ONE SOUL. Materializations only for the gratification of one or more egos never last or result in optimal happiness because they exclude the Happiness of the rest of their SELF, THE ONE SOUL. This is the way many who have forgotten who they are and who we all are choose to live on this earth. This is a mistaken way of life.

THE ONE SOUL, The TRUE SELF desires its own Happiness and the Happiness of All of the rest of SELF, the rest of Creation, because THE SELF, THE ONE SOUL REMEMBERS IT IS ONE. So a practical pointer is this. When You manifest, manifest Happiness for Yourself, for All those You love, and for ALL of creation. In this way, You have risen above the limited selfish ego, and remembered Who You really are, The Absolute, The All that You see with your physical eyes and the infinity which we cannot see with our physical eyes. The ego lives in separation and thinks that All others are separate from You, when in reality they are YOU.

If someone appears in your life, the person has appeared for a reason, to help you with your manifestation and make themSELF Happy in the process. All encounters You experience in Life happen for a reason, if they are for a moment, for a day, for a week, for a few years or for a lifetime. The appearance of these people is choreographed by the Youniverse, THE ONE SOUL, US ALL, IN ESSENCE. Explore the meaning of each encounter. Ask the person about their work, their passions. Nine times out of 10 You and they fit together somehow as puzzle pieces of Your and/or their materializations. THE ONE SOUL, of which You are an integral part, has delivered to You a puzzle piece of your materialization, another Divine person. The Universe rearranges itself, and put an interior puzzle piece (person) together with a second puzzle piece (2nd person), and then another (3rd person), and then another in a different location to assist You in Your and their materializations. The Universe operates at the speed of thought in the puzzle image manifestation as we have described above, completely non-linearly until the entire image that is Your materialization is reassembled. This is the beauty and the power of the Universe. So in terms of Your manifestations, when the opportunity to meet a new person or impulse arises, ACT NOW. Move with rapid action. The Universe has already rearranged itself for YOUR manifestation, putting in place all the money, people, events, connections, whatever is required for the 3-D realization; each encounter being one piece of Your puzzle. Be aware of all the instances for Action the Universe is setting in front of You for Your manifestation. If someone approaches you, start a discussion. Tell them about your manifestation. Ask them about their wishes. You shall be shocked and completely dazzled at the synchronous meetings that appear for You. The synchronous meetings are the domain of miracles, the Universe acting in concert with You and all Your other parts to bring about the Fastest, Happiest, Most Harmonious result for ALL.

Chapter 25

"If you love someone, set them free. If you wish them back, cast a spell on them fueled by unconditional love. They are destined to return."

Merlin

MATERIALIZING HARMONIOUS, HAPPY RELATIONSHIPS.

To materialize harmonious, happy relationships, You must first be in harmony and happy with Your Self. YOU MUST BE ALLONE FIRST. YOU MUST REMEMBER THAT YOU ARE THE CREATOR, UNCONDITIONAL LOVE FIRST. NO ONE MAKES YOU WHOLE, ALLONE. ONLY YOU REMEMBER WHO YOU ARE. At this point, the Law of Creation/Attraction operates to have All people you encounter and the experiences with these people be in harmony with you and to be happy with You. The way the Law of Creation/Attraction works is summarized as follows: 1) A person who lives from her/his

SOUL almost 100 percent of the time attracts the same person. This is a perfect harmonious, happy relationship. We call these folks: SOULFRIENDS. 2) SOULFRIENDS avoid/are not attracted to/leave mindfools. The vibrational level of these two groups of people vary significantly e.g., high vibe, unconditional love vs. low vibe, negative energy, ego. They are repelled from each other like the two similar poles of a magnet. 3) Mindfools attract mindfools. These are the relationships that are disharmonious and are to be avoided. These are the violent, abusive relationships that one reads about in the tabloids and newspapers, sees on television, and observes in real life. The relationships were created because of the vibrational energy of each of the individuals in the relationship and the fact that the law of attraction delivers an exact match to how they are feeling at any given time. THESE LAWS OF THE UNIVERSE HOLD TRUE FOR ALL RELATIONSHIPS E.G., FAMILY, FRIENDS, BUSINESS PARTNERS, HUSBAND AND WIFE, BOYFRIEND AND GIRLFRIEND, PARENTS/CHILDREN. THE TRUTHS IN LIFE ON EARTH ARE ALWAYS SIMPLE AS ARE THE SOLUTIONS TO THE MOST COMPLEX PUZZLES IN THE UNIVERSE.

Second, let's understand who the other person is in a relationship with you, be it family, friend, business partner, romantic acquaintance, person on the street, etc., IT IS YOU. Yes, the other person is simply YOU in a different form, with a different name, ultimately having a different life experience. What looks like a separate being, at the level of Spirit, is You. What you see with your physical eyes (the separate body of the other person) is an illusion in our 3-D earth plane. The illusion is duality, separateness, and difference, where in reality there is none. The realization that the other person is you has profound ramifications for how You think about, feel towards, and act towards another person. What would you intend and do for yourself and to yourself? Only things that make you happy. Right? So when you interact with another person, YOU in a different form, treat them the way you would treat yourself. You already love yourself. You are ready to Love all people You meet now. To materialize happy relationships, You must first create the right relationship with Your Self. You must love Your Self unconditionally. Then You create that which You wish to have mirrored back to You in a relationship.

WHAT DOES IT MEAN TO RISE IN LOVE? FIRST, LET US UNDERSTAND WHAT IT MEANS TO fall in love. Falling in love is the phrase that most humans use for a romantic relationship. It means two hearts having feelings for each other. But let's look at the meaning behind the words. Fall, means to fall down, trip up. This is not something desireable at all. It is an experience that happens at the level of the mind and body. The mind activates the emotions of passion, lust, puppy love, infatuation e.g., an interest in some aspect of the other that is appealing on the physical or intellectual level at best. It is a fleeting, temporary interest. **RISING IN LOVE IS WHAT IS TRUE LOVE. IT IS A UNION THAT RISES ABOVE THE DESIRES OF THE** mind and body, yet the **UNION INCLUDES THE** mind and body as we are tripartite **BEINGS IN EARTHLY INCARNATIONS**, mind, body and Soul. **RISING IN LOVE IS THE UNION OF TWO SOULS BACK INTO THE ONENESS, UNCONDITIONAL LOVE. OUR ORIGINAL AND REAL STATE. THIS IS WHERE YOU WISH TO BE.** All else is "love" in the illusion, temporary, fading.

Chapter 26

"People who create their own drama, deserve their own Karma."

Anonymous

UNDERSTANDING THE LAW OF KARMA, PART II: ITS RELATIONSHIP TO LOVING YOURSELF.

What is another way to understand Karma? Karma is baggage, both beautiful bags and ugly bags that you carry with You at the Spiritual level that reflect into 3-D earthly experiences in one lifetime or across lifetimes. How does the Law of Karma function in relation to how You Love Youself, and Why? Its really very simple. If You Love Yourself in a Very Healthy way, You create beautiful bags of Karma for you to carry. By the Law of Attraction, your beautiful Karmic bags grow, and you are blessed with a life of comfort and love. The opposite holds true also. If you fail to love yourself, then you create ugly bags on your travels in the current life and in other lives.

Similarly, if you are a person living and believing in the illusion of duality, separation, and if You are intending and doing negative things to another person, You are really intending and doing them to yourself e.g., creating and carrying ugly Karmic bags. Hence, create beautiful Karmic bags of love and happiness for yourself and all others. This only makes sense, since you are doing ALL good things for the SELF, and as we ALL remember there is ONLY ONE SELF.

Chapter 27

HOW TO MATERIALIZE HARMONIOUS RELATIONSHIPS FROM disharmonic ones; CLEANSING KARMA FROM RELATIONSHIPS.

Disharmonic relationships are for Us to understand who We are NOT. FIRST, WE ARE ONLY UNCONDITIONAL LOVE AT THE LEVEL OF SOUL. The illusory mask/ego only serves to show US ALL WHO WE ARE NOT, and creates all disharmonic relationships. Life at the level of ego/mask is disharmonic e.g., out of tune. It is an experience of Life in the illusion of separation. This is Why people speak about, harm, avoid, and generally treat others with negativity, unkindness. From the perspective of relationships, our earlier definition of the types of beings on earth can be further simplified: there are only two types of people here on planet Earth with respect to relationships: 1) People who are UNMASKED, who remember who they are, who You are, THE ONE SOUL,

UNCONDITIONAL LOVE in a human costume, and 2) People who are masked and who forget who they are, and who You are. It is that simple. With this understanding, harmonius relationships are created by unmasking the mask wearers. That is, by helping the mask wearers remember who we ALL ARE, THE ONE SOUL, UNCONDITIONAL LOVE.

The mask wearers' thoughts, feelings, and actions can be understood with a glass and water analogy: "You only drink as much water as is already in a glass. A full glass results in a completely refreshing drink. With an empty glass, you are always left thirsty." So it is with relationships with mask wearers, the other can only offer You that which She or He already is full of e.g., low vibing energy, jealousy, superficiality, egoism. So ask Yourself, what is the person across from You full of? Goodness? Unconditional Love? Or something else? Is that person an empty glass or something in-between which may not be completely satisfying? Most importantly, are you a full or empty glass of Unconditional Love? If You and the person sitting across from You are a full glass of unconditional love, smiles, happiness, by the Law of Creation/Attraction, You and they attract the same in Your Lives, and have a harmonious relationship.

Temporary mask wearers in disharmonic relationships do serve a purpose. They show us and themselves who we are NOT. To elaborate further, let's look at the Chinese Yin and the Yang, The contrast and The Light, the black and the white. Some people through their forgetfulness live contrast and project contrast onto the lives of the people they interact with. They are the people who don't respond or smile to You when You smile or say Hello to them. They treat you strangely e.g., where the meaning of the word stranger comes from. They simply have forgotten who they are and who You are. Their actions do serve an important purpose for You: They show You how You are NOT to ACT. Without the contrast, you would not know that You are The Light and how to act according to who You really are.

How should I react when a person treats me strangely? There are a couple of really sane options and an insane option. First the insane option; react to them as they acted toward you. This option is insane since it creates escalating conflict and negative energy, which by The Law of Attraction then feeds upon itself and grows. They treat you strangely, you treat them strangely, and the cycle perpetuates e.g., where the meaning of the word stranger comes from. The sane option is to remember who they really are and who You are, unconditional love, and throw that Love back at them. This breaks the cycle of negativity, causes a harmonius relationship to materialize, and cleans up Karma. The Karma may have been created between You and the other in this lifetime, or may have been created between the parties in previous lifetimes and residually passed into an experience in Your current lifetime. Throwing Love into the experience also neutralizes the negative energy they has been thrown off since its energy is orders of magnitude stronger energetically than the negative.

You should help the other to remember who they are and who you are, with words and actions also, in addition to your feelings and intentions. In this way you are helping YOUR SELF, in the other physical form, remembering who they are and who you are. You are helping yourself. Applying the "I AM" LAW OF NATURE causes harmonious relationships to materialize. When faced with a person who attacks you or is unpleasant to you, react with a smile and kind words and tell them: I AM YOU and YOU ARE ME. This cleans up the Karma. Watch what happens as the person's Spirit instantly realizes the Truth and cages their ego that caused the negative situation in the first place. This works each and every time. This was the reason Jesus Christ taught: "Love GOD (YOURSELF) with All Your Heart, Love Your Neighbor as Yourself." He understood that the Neighbor is the SELF, and there is ONLY ONE SELF, GOD, YOU, THE ONE SOUL, UNCONDITIONAL LOVE.

Another technique to materialize harmonious relationships where there is disharmony is to send continuous positive energy to the person in disharmony. This is accomplished by positive focused "spell casting." The Spell takes the form of a Mantra that You recite and believe is already done. For example, "I AND (NAME THE PERSON) ALIGN ALL OF MY THOUGHTS, FEELINGS, WORDS, AND ACTIONS TO SERVE MY BEST AND HIGHEST GOOD AND THAT OF ALL AROUND US. I AND (NAME THE PERSON) ARE UNCONDITIONAL LOVE FOR OUR SELVES, FOR EACH OTHER, AND FOR ALL AROUND US." This is a powerful positive spell. Write it down. Recite it. Feel it is done. Put it in a prominent place where You see it all the time, and repeat the process until it is done 3-D. White witch/warlock-craft works 100 percent of the time.

Chapter 28

HOW TO MATERIALIZE HEALTH AND HEALING IN YOUR LIFE AND THE LIVES OF OTHERS: THE NATURAL LAW OF SELF-HEALING.

Like any other manifestation/materialization, physical health is a materialization which You call forth, and the Youniverse, YOU, THE ONE SOUL rearranges all cells and tissues within your physical body for you to enjoy that experience. This is called The Natural Law of Self-Healing. Be grateful for the healthy body that Your Spirit animates. Be HAPPY all the time. By the Law of Attraction, more health, as an experience, manifests for You to enjoy. Be laughter, smiles, and worry-free Happiness. Enjoy Sports, Yoga, Natural Foods, walking in Nature, Spirit to Spirit sex, whatever brings You individually and All around you happiness. The Youniverse is ALL intelligence, and Your physical body reacts to the intentions You set forth for Yourself. In this way, **YOU SELF-HEAL ALL AILMENTS USING THE NATURAL LAW OF SELF-HEALING.**

A good general rule is to avoid establishment medicine as much as possible, except for traumatic injury. Although there are individuals who entered the field of medicine for altruistic reasons, as the medical industry has evolved, it has become a farce. Despite many instances where medical intervention does achieve positive results, it is rarely the most efficient or best way to treat a human problem of DIS-EASE. The Medical industry is about making money and little more. Pills are developed to treat symptoms and often they work at that level, but rarely remove the causes of the symptoms. A better approach is to remember who You truly are. Until the root cause of the illness is addressed and the Spirit is AT EASE, the opposite of dis-ease, the contrast in Life, a patient is not truly cured. So no matter what physical affliction you suffer, remember who You are, The Creator, and You have brought on this health experience into Your Life to help You remember who You are. Materialize a SELF-HEALING FOR YOUR SELF as part of Your Life experience. The Cure is as simple as the condition, and You cure yourself by the I AM therapy: Intention, Action (Easing the Spirit), Materialization of Health. This includes the use of remedies that are found in Nature, and results in a Manifestation of Health. Health is a delicious miracle a NATURAL-BORN MIRACLE MAKER enjoys.

Chapter 29

"Don't grieve. Anything you lose comes around in another form."

Rumi

THE NATURAL LAWS OF RESURRECTION AND REINCARNATION; THE MIRACLES OF ANIMATION OF RE-ANIMATION OF A PHYSICAL BODY.

To understand Your Life, remember what death is. Death is an illusion. What is A REAL FACT is that YOUR SOUL, THE ONE SOUL, GOD, IS ALIVE AS YOU IN THE PRESENT ETERNAL NOW, ALWAYS. Death is the de-animation of your physical body by Your Soul, THE ONE SOUL. In other words, Your SOUL leaves your body, and your body returns to dust. After Your ETERNAL SOUL de-animates your body, YOU DO A LIFE SELF-REVIEW OF YOUR PAST INCARNATION. AS DESCRIBED BY MANY SOULS WHO HAVE de-animated their bodies and then re-animated them, RESURRECTED

(THE SOUL RETURNING TO THE SAME BODY), YOU SEE AND FEEL YOUR ENTIRE LIFE, SCENE BY SCENE, INSTANTLY. YOU FEEL ALL THAT YOU FELT WHILE IN YOUR BODY AND FEEL THE FEELINGS OF ALL YOU HAVE ENCOUNTERED IN YOUR PREVIOUS LIFE E.G., CHILDREN, PARENTS, FRIENDS, FAMILY, AND THE "stranger on the street." The reason this happens is that the REALITY is, WE ARE ALL ONE SOUL, THE CREATOR, LOOKING AT ITSELF, AND THE EXPERIENCES YOU CREATED (MATERIALIZED) HAD AN EFFECT ON YOU AND THE REST OF YOU E.G., THE ILLUSORY OTHER SOULS.

ONCE YOUR SOUL IS LIBERATED FROM THE RULES THAT GOVERN EARTHLY INCARNATIONS, ONE OF SEVERAL THINGS HAPPEN: 1) YOU REINCORPORATE INTO THE ONE SOUL, IF YOU HAVE REMEMBERED IN YOUR EARTHLY INCARNATION THAT YOU ARE THE ONE SOUL, UNCONDITIONAL LOVE; 2) YOU RESURRECT. YOUR SOUL RE-ANIMATES THE SAME BODY IF YOUR WORK IN THAT BODY (YOUR SOUL MISSION) IS INCOMPLETE. Many examples of resurrection are in literature e.g., JESUS CHRIST, LAZURUS, and many others. JESUS CHRIST'S LIFE MISSION, REMEMBERING THAT HE AND WE ALL ARE THE ONE SOUL, WAS

TO SHOW US THIS FACT: "LOOK YOU ALL, THEY (the mindfooled) CRUCIFIED ME AND MURDERED ME. I AM AS YOU ARE, THE CREATOR. I CHOSE TO RISE FROM THE DEAD, AND DO." SO, JESUS CHRIST "SAVES" MANY FROM THE IGNORANCE OF FORGETTING THAT WE ALL ARE LESS THAN THE CREATOR; 3) THE THIRD THING WE CHOOSE TO HAPPEN AFTER A SELF-"LIFE ASSESSMENT," RECOGNIZING THAT IN A LIFETIME WE FAILED TO REMEMBER THAT WE ARE THE CREATOR, UNCONDITIONAL LOVE, IS THAT WE REINCARNATE; 4) THE FOURTH THING WE MAY CHOOSE TO DO IS TO RETURN TO THE ILLUSION OF SEPARATE SOULS AND REINCARNATE TO ACCOMPLISH ANOTHER SOUL MISSION, SUCH AS PLANETARY CHANGE ON THIS EARTH, RETURN TO THE EARTH TO PARADISE.

REINCARNATION IS A SOUL CHOOSING TO ANIMATE A PHYSICAL FORM AS A NEWLY BORN BABY CHILD. The author, remembering he is THE ONE SOUL, AND AT ONE WITH ALL OF YOU, AND INDEED ALL CREATION SEEN AND UNSEEN, has a marvelous gift in this life. If the author sees a pregnant woman, he can tell her if she is going to have a baby boy or girl with 99.5 percent accuracy. NOW ANOTHER SYNCHRONOUS EVENT JUST TRANSPIRED.

PERFECT TIMING. At the time of this writing and as the author just stepped out to smoke his cigar on Lake Zurich in Switzerland, the next reincarnation synchrodestiny appeared for Czeslawa Ziarno (died 12 6, 1986, as described above) that reincarnated in 1995: a BMW MINI Cooper was along the path the author walked with the plate: 1 95 12 6, soon followed by a birth year 1961 car license plate; synchronicity for the reincarnation of the author's American Patent Attorney and Inventor friend, James D. B., appeared. Many of our talents from previous lives transfer to subsequent lives. In the case of Nikola Tesla, he was an amazing inventor who developed many of the technologies which we enjoy everyday including wireless technologies, etc. Nikola Tesla was reincarnated as James D. B. in this life continuing to use his talents as an extremely accomplished and prolific inventor and electrical engineer.

SOULS RETURN IN SOUL FAMILIES, EACH SOUL FAMILY MEMBER AGREEING TO SPECIFIC ROLES AND MAJOR LIFE EVENTS WHILE IN THE SPIRIT REALM. In one life you may be another soul's mother, son, grandfather, uncle, friend, girlfriend, wife, pet cat or dog, or husband. In another life, the roles are changed. THE FACT is that All of Us have lived many lives or incarnations, each incarnation serving the purpose of US remembering WE ARE THE

CREATOR, UNCONDITIONAL LOVE. Some incarnations have greater lessons and richer content and remembrances, some lesser.

This Author has documented (VIA THE NATURAL LAW OF SYNCHRONICITY, DREAMS, VISIONS, AND OTHER METHODS) his previous major incarnations, and the major incarnations of those in his SOUL FAMILY which appear in the feature films released by I AM STUDIO PRODUCTIONS AG. This author, also via the Natural Laws of Synchronicity and Synchrodestiny, documented the upcoming reincarnations of specific members of his Soul family, and has already predicted the incarnation of a major historical Soul, St. Thomas the Apostle. These are the facts around the current incarnation of brother St. Thomas the Apostle. The author's girlfriend Alina in Dnipropetrovsk, Ukraine is the reinarnation of the author's best childhood friend, Albert, who passed away in that life at the age of 23 being born in 1963. Alina was born in 1993 and met the author synchronistically in 2011 as she served as a hostess at a medical congress for the author's start-up medical device company in female healthcare (Lumeden e.g., Light Medicine). Alina then left the author and started a relationship with another individual while she still kept in touch with the author via Skype. Alina then found herself pregnant. We exchanged Skype messages with Alina without her telling us anything about the marriage or her pregnancy. During the Skype message, the author intuitively felt the Soul of the unborn child Alina was carrying, told her it was to be a boy (which it was), and then subsequently told Alina that the boy was the incarnation of St. Thomas the Apostle. The author mentions another synchronicity for this incarnation in that the author visited the grave of St. Thomas the Apostle in Chennai, India while the author worked as a Director at a large outsourcing company based in New York, London, and India (Office Tiger, acquired by Chicago based RR Donnelley). With respect to all the worlds You see when You look up at the Trillions of Galaxies in the night sky, incarnations are also chosen by You in a variety of other Star systems and galaxies, as well as Angelic incarnations in higher nonphysical dimensions depending on Your SOUL'S CHOSEN PATH. As such, the silliest act a human can do is grieve at a funeral of a loved one. Why? THAT SOUL, THE ONE SOUL, GOD ITSELF, LIVES FOREVER IN THE ETERNAL PRESENT MOMENT, AND MAY CHOOSE TO REINCARNATE INTO HUMAN FORM AGAIN IN A SOUL FAMILY SO THEY ARE ONCE AGAIN TOGETHER IN CORPOREAL FORM HERE ON EARTH AND ELSEWHERE.

Chapter 30

"Important encounters are planned by souls long before the bodies see each other."

Paulo Coelho

"[B]elieve...and [You] will do even greater things than these."

Jesus Christ

THE MIRACLES OF SOUL FAMILY CREATION AND SOUL FAMILY REUNIONS VIA REINCARNATION.

Those who remember they are THE ONE SOUL, THE CREATOR, UNCONDITIONAL LOVE, are poised to work Miracles on an unprecedented scale which those who have incarnated on this planet Earth have not yet seen before. Miracles as great and greater than those of Jesus Christ and other Ascended Masters are Yours for the creation as Natural-born Miracle

Makers. These Miracles include calling forth INCARNATIONS of ASCENDED MASTER SOULS, STAR CHILDREN FROM OTHER GALAXIES, ARCHANGELS from other realms and Star systems, and those who have heretofor REINTEGRATED INTO THE ONE SOUL, THE LIGHT. THE AUTHOR HAS NOW MET IN HUMAN FORM MANY NOW ON EARTH WHO HAVE EXPERIENCED HISTORICAL INCARNATIONS IN MAJOR POLITICAL, RELIGIOUS, BUSINESS, ENTERTAINMENT, TECHNOLOGICAL, AND OTHER IMPORTANT SECTORS. The Souls currently incarnate now include: Moses, Miriam, Moses' sister, Cleopatra, Marcus Antonius, St. Veronika, St. Andrew the Apostle, St. Thomas the Apostle, Mary Magdalene, St. Joan of Arc, Sultan Suleiman, Hurrem Sultan, The Buddha, Nikola Tesla, John Jacob Astor, Marilyn Monroe, one of Marcus Antonius' Roman generals, the three Buddhist Monks who arrived at the birth of Jesus Christ, Judas Iscariot, Octavian, and many others. Other historical Souls incarnating include Jesus Christ, St. Paul the Apostle, St. Phillip the Apostle, and many, many others. The author has remembered his previous historical incarnations and they shall be presented in feature films with the objective of Entertaining the Souls of Us All with the Truth, as well as to get the messages of Truth concerning reincarnation into the Western World where humanity has been erroneously conditioned to think that we each have only one life, and that We All are somehow less than the CREATOR, THE ONE SOUL, UNCONDITIONAL LOVE.

The objectives of these Soul's incarnations with many, many others (Our Collective Soul Mission) is to lead what we have termed the Earth's Return to Paradise, back to an Age of Remembering who WE ALL ARE sans the contrast created by the limited, overactive ego, returning humanity back to an Age of Innocence. The Lives of these legendary SOULS ARE PORTRAYED IN OUR QUADRILOGY OF FEATURE FILMS: *The Contrast, The Light, Return to Paradise* and *The Absolute* to help the mass audience remember who they are, who we ALL ARE. The author has also chronicled for the historical record the synchronicities for the previous lives of many other historically important Souls who incarnate in the Earth's Return to Paradise.

A further power you all have as NATURAL-BORN MIRACLE MAKERS is that You may materialize the children You wish to be in Your immediate family here on earth. How and Why? You are THE CREATOR. By way of example, one of the co-stars in the NATURAL-BORN MIRACLE MAKERS film shared with us the true story around the birth of his second child. The co-star was travelling on business when his wife delivered his first child, and because of the business trip he missed being with his wife for the birth of their first child. The co-star and his wife decided to have a second child, and this time the co-star called forth the sex of the child and also the date when the child would be born so that he could organize his professional travel schedule around this date, and be at his child's birth. Of course, all materialized as called forth. **He is a NATURAL-BORN MIRACLE MAKER.** The author also recalls a true story one of his friends in St. Gallen, Switzerland shared with him. The friend is a very Spiritually attuned Swiss gentlemen, with a Brazilian ex-wife. They had a first boy together, and then wished for a second son. Our Swiss friend called forth a second son who would be very Spiritually and artistically gifted. The Swiss friend engaged in Mantra chanting and using the I AM principle. His wish was granted and the second son fit the request perfectly. He has a wonderfully close relationship with his father and they enjoy photography, music video creation, nature walks, and other events together. It is also possible to call forth and materialize the exact children You have in Your family using the I AM principle. Result is 100 percent guarenteed. Those who are Spiritually "untuned" may tell You this is impossible. They are mistaken because they have forgotten who we ALL are.

Chapter 31

"Nowhere can a man find a quieter and untroubled retreat than in his own soul."
Marcus Antonius

HOW TO LIVE A BEAUTIFUL LIFE AS A NATURAL-BORN MIRACLE MAKER; PRACTICAL MIRACLES.

Now we share with you specific steps, for You as A NATURAL BORN MIRACLE MAKER, THE CREATOR, to use in your earthly incarnations to materialize a beautiful human incarnation experience. First remember, the ONLY two purposes You have here in human form are: 1) TO REMEMBER YOU ARE THE CREATOR, THE ONE SOUL, IN A HUMAN COSTUME, UNCONDITIONAL LOVE, AND THAT ALL AROUND YOU IS ANOTHER FORM OF YOU IN A DIFFERENT COSTUME, AND 2) TO BE HAPPY WHATEVER HAPPINESS MEANS FOR YOU AND ALL AROUND YOU AT THE SAME TIME. The steps below are shared with those for which Happiness is augmented with certain 3-D experiences (as they remember that they are ALL HAPPINESS WITHIN ALREADY). Each of You individually knows which experiences are Happy for You. As such, You may wish to tailor Your materializations using the principles described below.

Choose to tune Yourself first in Spirituality and Self-improvement. When You are tuned, you are ready to assist others around You to tune themselves. Tuning means to bring Your Self up to the highest state of Happiness that is right for You. You tune Yourself by Loving Your Self and others around You simultaneously. Tune Yourself by choosing to BE HAPPY ALL THE TIME. Feel and BE the Beauty You already are. Make Your Mind Your SOUL'S Servant Through Meditation/Yoga/any practice that brings you into a state of thought-less-ness. Materialize a Fit Body through intention and action: Visualization, Diet, and Fitness. Wear Fashion or Go Naked. Do that which Makes You Feel Good. BE AND LIVE IN THE PRESENT MOMENT ONLY AS YOUR MATERIALIZATIONS PROCEED THROUGH 3-D PROCESS. TUNE OTHERS AROUND YOU BY USING THE I AM PRINCIPLE FOR THEIR BEST AND HIGHEST GOOD, AND THAT OF THE ALL. TUNE YOUR SURROUNDINGS, EXTENSIONS OF YOU TO SUPPORT YOUR MATERIALIZATIONS. YOUR

SURROUNDINGS ARE EXTENSIONS OF YOU. MATERIALIZE CONTINUAL EXPERIENCES WITH POSITIVE SOULS (BOYFRIENDS, GIRLFRIENDS, HUSBANDS, WIVES, CHILDREN, FRIENDS, ETC.), WHO VIBE AT THE SAME POSITIVE LEVEL YOU DO. BE ALLONE WITH YOUR SELF THROUGHOUT THE DAY, IN EVERY MOMENT. Being AllOne means feeling the ONENESS OF ALL CREATION WITH YOU. AVOID EXPERIENCES WITH BEINGS WHO VIBE AT LOWER LEVELS OF HAPPINESS e.g., live in the illusion of separation because of their masks.

Choose to tune Your surroundings e.g., Your home and Your place of work. Tuning Your surroundings involves using the vision boarding process to infuse Your home and workplace with high vibrational energy. First, it is best to clean out existing or residual energies in Your home or workplace. This is done with the ritual of Your choice calling forth the removal of all energies that fail to serve your best and highest good and that of all the other Souls inhabiting or visiting Your home or workplace. Next, infuse the place with super-high vibing positive energy using the techniques described herein. This is a materialization like any other. Call forth that All beings entering Your home and workplace are happy and super-positive. Invoke these energies at your entrance door: "I CALL FORTH

THAT ALL PEOPLE COMING THROUGH MY FRONT DOOR BRING WITH THEM SUPER-POSITIVE HAPPY ENERGY INTO MY HOME (OR WORKPLACE) TO SERVE THE BEST AND HIGHEST GOOD OF ALL OF OUR SOULS. SO IT IS DONE."

Choose to tune the other people in Your life or coming into Your life. This is a form of Spell casting using the I AM principle and can be termed a form of White Goddess/Wizard craft, because it is. At its core, it is no more than another form of materialization of an experience in Your life with other beings. This is energy work, so recharge Yourself after You are done. Cast a spell on each person as follows—You may also use a photo of them and vision board the spell on the photo: "I AM (NAME OF THE PERSON) AND ENJOY BEING UNCONDITIONAL LOVE, HAPPINESS, AND LAUGHTER WITH (YOUR NAME) IN A WAY THAT SERVES THE BEST AND HIGHEST GOOD OF MY SOUL AND ALL THE SOULS AROUND ME. SO IT IS DONE."

Why do these tuning methods work? They work because the other is really YOU in another costume, so at the end of the day, You are really tuning Yourself even though the illusion makes it appear that You are tuning another person, place, or thing. The results of these tuning methods are truly amazing and the author has documented hundreds of examples of how these methods work. Just last night as the author was writing this work, our friend, Achim, returned from a short shopping trip to Zurich. Upon his return he commented to us that he got his 18 year old positive groove back (he is now 41). He says he lost it for a period of time. What happened? Two things. First, the energy we are currently emanating is very high vibing. We are vibing at Unconditional Love, Oneness. Achim also has a really positive vibration. We also cast a spell on his place and him of Happiness. All of our words and actions were aligned with our intention. We charged him and his place up with positive energy. Results materialized successfully.

Chapter 32

> "Your soul is your connection to the Divine. Sacred sex is an activity of joining souls in holy, celestial creation, expressing your appreciation for the gift of life, of sharing your body's vitality with another."
> Brownell Landrum

LET'S TALK ABOUT SEX: SACRED ENERGY EXCHANGE, MATERIALIZING SOULGASMS.

Sex is a Sacred Act. SEX means Sacred Energy Xchange, and it is a powerful energy tool for accelerating the materialization process as we have described above. As with All powerful tools, it is used wisely. We all have energy bodies that extend three meters outside of our physical forms forming part of the ONE ENERGY THAT IS US ALL, THE ONE SOUL. As such, when we are intimate with another person, our energy bodies overlap and absorb the other's energy. Nowhere is this more powerful than in the expression of sexual love alongside OUR NATURAL STATE OF UNCONDITIONAL LOVE, OUR VERY ESSENCE. THE OBJECTIVE IS TO HAVE ALL CHAKRAS UNITE (with Your Partner(s)), AND HAVE A POSITIVE FLOW OF ENERGY EXCHANGE BETWEEN THE FEMALE AND MALE AT THE SPIRITUAL AND PHYSICAL LEVEL. This is accomplished by visualization and physical techniques: 1) Continuous EYE (Physical and Third Eye) contact between Lovers. EYES are the physical and Spiritual windows to the Soul; 2) BE One with Your Lover's SOUL IN THE MOMENT. Both Minds off. Pure Soul to Soul Interaction; 3) Energy flow: All Chakra Light Energies flowing from One Lover through the Other Lover; 4) Surroundings: As You Like them. Energize them positively prior to the sacred sexual union; 5) Create a sensory atmosphere for Soul to Soul Love. Aromas, Lighting (Candles), Music, Comfort; 6) Materialize Multiple Soulgasms. Reunite both Souls through intention; 7) Loving Action. Kama Sutra Positions flowing spontaneously and naturally as each other likes; 8) Afterplay. Enjoying relaxing teas, fruits, meditation. Falling asleep in a tender embrace with your Lover; and 9) Zero Out: a) All that is other than Natural e.g., birth control, gels, etc., and b) All that disturbs the Sacred Union e.g., outside distractions.

Sacred energy exchange involves MAKING LOVE WITH A WOMBMAN'S AND A MAN'S SOUL. THIS MATERIALIZES SOULGASMS. SOULGASMS ARE THE EXTENDED UNION OF TWO SOULS IN PERFECT ECTASY. ALL CHAKRAS UNITED AS THE ONE SOUL, UNCONDITIONAL LOVE. AS YOU CAN IMAGINE, SOULGASMS ARE EXPERIENCED ONLY BETWEEN TWO PARTNERS WHO ARE VIBING AT A LEVEL OF UNCONDITIONAL LOVE FOR EACH OTHER. By way of contrast, lower vibing root chakra orgasms are experienced by those who vibe at that low energetic level. IF ONE PARTNER VIBES AT THE LEVEL OF SOULGASMS and the other at the low vibing root chakra level, the low viber acts as an energy vampire and drains the SOULGASMER'S SOULGASM Energy.

Chapter 33

"Let it be done."
                Cleopatra VII, Queen of Egypt

YOU ARE THE CREATOR, A NATURAL-BORN MIRACLE MAKER: CONCLUSORY ACTIONS.

1. BE THE UNCONDITIONAL LOVE THAT YOU ALREADY ARE.
2. BE PRESENT IN THE ETERNAL NOW ALWAYS.
3. FORGET THE PAST, IT ISN'T REAL.
4. THINK NOT OF THE FUTURE. IT ALSO ISN'T REAL.
5. BE THAT WHICH YOU WISH TO EXPERIENCE NOW.
6. VISUALIZE THAT WHICH YOU WISH TO EXPERIENCE.
7. REMEMBER: YOU ARE ONE WITH ALL AROUND YOU.
8. BEING ONE WITH ALL AROUND YOU MEANS YOU LOVE YOURSELF AND

ALL THAT IS YOU AROUND YOU UNCONDITIONALLY.
9. CREATE ABUNDANCE OF ALL GOOD THINGS USING THE I AM PRINCIPLE FOR YOURSELF.
10. SHARE THE ABUNDANCE YOU MATERIALIZE WITH ALL AROUND YOU GENEROUSLY.
11. REMEMBER, THE MORE GENEROUS YOU ARE, THE MORE ABUNDANCE THE ONE SOUL, THE REST OF YOU, MIRRORS BACK TO YOU.
12. USE SEX, SACRED ENERGY EXCHANGE, AS A TOOL TO ENJOY THE OTHER PARTS OF YOU IN A WHOLE UNION.
13. BE ALLONE, BE WHOLE WITHIN YOURSELF WHEN ENTERING INTO ANY RELATIONSHIP WITH ANOTHER.
14. REMEMBER THAT YOU ARE SACRED AND ALL AROUND YOU ARE SACRED PEOPLE, PLANTS, ANIMALS, AIR, WATER, AND THE EARTH ITSELF.
15. REMEMBER THAT YOU HAVE LIVED MANY TIMES BEFORE.
16. REMEMBER THAT ALL MATERIALIZATIONS HAPPEN AT THE LEVEL OF CREATION FIRST AND

THEN GO THROUGH AN INEVITABLE 3-D PROCESS.
17. REMEMBER THAT 100 PERCENT OF YOUR INTENTIONS MATERIALIZE AT THE PERFECT TIME.
18. REMEMBER YOU CREATE YOUR OWN REALITY.
19. REMEMBER NOT TO WORRY ABOUT THE OPINIONS OF ANYONE WEARING A MASK HAS ABOUT YOU.
20. REMEMBER THAT YOU ONLY TEMPORARILY ANIMATE YOUR PHYSICAL BODY.
21. REMEMBER THAT RESURRECTION AND REINCARNATION ARE LAWS OF NATURE.
22. REMEMBER THAT SYNCHRONICITY IS A NATURAL LAW.
23. FOLLOW SYNCHRONICITIES TO GUIDE YOU TO THE END RESULT OF YOUR MATERIALIZATIONS.
24. MAKE YOUR END RESULT YOUR DESTINY BY INSTANTLY ACTING ON SYNCHRONICITIES TO CREATE YOUR SYNCHRODESTINY, FATE.
25. TAKE ALL MATERIALIZATIONS TO THE END RESULT.
26. FINANCIAL MATERIALIZATIONS ARE LIKE ANY OTHER MATERIALIZATION

AND FLOW TO YOU EASILY AND EFFORTLESSLY.
27. USE VISUALIZATION TO FEEL YOU ALREADY ARE WHERE YOU WISH TO BE NOW.
28. FEEL GRATITUDE FOR ALL THE GOODNESS IN YOUR LIFE.
29. REMEMBER THE NATURAL LAW OF MIRRORING AND USE IT.
30. REMEMBER THE NATURAL LAW OF KARMA AND USE IT.
31. REMEMBER THE NATURAL LAW OF SELF-HEALING AND USE IT.
32. REMEMBER YOU ALREADY ARE ALL THAT YOU WISH TO EXPERIENCE HERE NOW.
33. REMEMBER THAT YOU ONLY HAVE TO DO TWO THINGS IN LIFE: 1) REMEMBER YOU ARE THE CREATOR, UNCONDITIONAL LOVE, AND 2) BE HAPPY, WHATEVER HAPPINESS MEANS FOR YOU AND ALL AROUND YOU SIMULTANEOUSLY.

www.ingramcontent.com/pod-product-compliance
Lightning Source LLC
LaVergne TN
LVHW020930090426
835512LV00020B/3304